THE OPEN UNIVERSITY
Social sciences: A third level cours
Social policy and social welfare

BLOCK 1
CONFLICT AND CONTROVERSY OVER WELFARE PROVISION

UNIT 2
IDEOLOGIES OF WELFARE: THE TURN OF THE CENTURY

UNIT 3
IDEOLOGIES OF WELFARE: THE MOMENT OF '1945'

UNIT 4
IDEOLOGIES OF WELFARE: INTO THE 1980s

The Open University Press

CORE COURSE TEAM

Martin Loney   *Lecturer in Social Policy/Course Team Chairperson/Unit author*
David Boswell   *Senior Lecturer in Sociology/Unit author*
John Clarke   *Lecturer in Social Policy/Unit author*
Carol Johns   *Secretary*
Jennie Pawson   *Course manager*

OTHER OPEN UNIVERSITY CONTRIBUTORS

Andy Blowers   *Senior Lecturer in Geography/Unit author*
Francis G. Castles   *Reader in Political Science/Unit author*
Gloria Channing   *Secretary*
Annie Clutterbuck   *Editor*
Allan Cochrane   *Lecturer in Urban Studies/Unit author*
Marie Day   *Secretary*
Richard Hoyle   *Designer*
Tom Hunter   *Editor*
Linda McDowell   *Lecturer in Geography/Unit author*
Gregor McLennan   *Research Fellow (Sociology)/Unit author*
Stella Pilsworth   *Liaison librarian*
Christopher Pollitt   *Lecturer in Government/Unit author*
Sonja Ruehl   *Lecturer in Economics/Unit author*
Francis Seeley   *Producer, BBC*
Eleanor Thompson   *Project Controller*
Chris Wooldridge   *Co-ordinating editor*

EXTERNAL AUTHORS

Michael Jackson   *Senior Lecturer in Social Administration, University of Stirling*
John Raine   *Lecturer at INLOGOV, Birmingham*
Carol Smart   *Research Sociologist, Institute of Psychiatry, London*
Peter Taylor-Gooby   *Lecturer in Social Policy, University of Kent*

EXTERNAL ASSESSORS

Louie Burghes (Unit 9)   *Research Worker, Low Pay Unit, London*
Vic George (Course assessor and Block 1)   *Professor of Social Policy, University of Kent*
Joan Higgins (Block 2)   *Lecturer in Social Administration, University of Southampton*
Richard Silburn (Block 3)   *Senior Lecturer in Social Administration, Nottingham University*
Adrian Webb (Block 4)   *Professor of Social Administration, Loughborough University*

We would also like to acknowledge the work of Maureen Adams, Doreen Beacham, Pat Cooke, Mary Dicker, Eve Hussey, Michelle Kent, Val Kirby and Iris Manzi who typed various units.

The Open University Press
Walton Hall, Milton Keynes
MK7 6AA

First published 1984

Copyright © 1984 The Open University

Designed by the Graphic Design Group of the Open University.

Printed in England by Dawson & Goodall Ltd, Bath.

ISBN 0 335 12171 3

This text forms part of an Open University course. The complete list of units in the course appears at the end of this text.

For general availability of supporting material referred to in this text, please write to Open University Educational Enterprises Limited, 12 Cofferidge Close, Stony Stratford, Milton Keynes, MK11 1BY, Great Britain.

Further information on Open University courses may be obtained from the Admissions Office, The Open University, P.O. Box 48, Walton Hall, Milton Keynes, MK7 6AB.

1.1

UNIT 2

IDEOLOGIES OF WELFARE: THE TURN OF THE CENTURY

Prepared for the Course Team by John Clarke, Allan Cochrane and Carol Smart

CONTENTS

1 INTRODUCTION TO IDEOLOGIES OF WELFARE

Unit 1 examined some of the conflicts and controversies through which the welfare state in Britain has developed, in Units 2, 3, and 4 we shall be considering one aspect of these conflicts in more detail. Unit 1 identified the welfare state as the object of competing ideologies, ideologies which involve views of the existing state provisions, views about what the state should do and what sorts of welfare provision should be available. In these units, it is our intention to look at these ideologies of welfare more closely: to view the sorts of controversies between different ideologies, to trace the development of different ideologies, and to examine the views of welfare and the state which they propound.

We have identified four main political ideologies which have had particularly strong connections with the development of the welfare state in Britain. By political ideologies we mean relatively developed systems of ideas and concepts which offer systematic accounts of the relationship between society, the state and welfare. The ideologies with which we are concerned here are both 'explanatory' and 'normative'. They provide explanations of the existing nature of welfare provision, and of what circumstances create a need for welfare provision (individual failings, economic inequalities and so on). But they are also 'normative': they contain a view of *what welfare should be* and *how it should be provided.*

We have identified them as *political* ideologies, but we must give a warning about our use of this term. These ideologies are not 'political' because they 'belong' to any one particular political party — 'laissez-faire' ideologies do not belong to the Conservative party, any more than 'socialism' belongs to the Labour party. These ideologies form a sort of ideological repertoire — an array of major themes and ideas — on which political parties have drawn at particular times. They are larger than their uses by parties, providing a system of ideas which shape the sphere of politics. We have chosen them precisely because they are broader (and have a longer and more persistent history) than party manifestoes. It could be said that these ideologies 'inform' the politics of welfare — parties and other groups involved in conflicts over welfare make reference to these broad systems of ideas, draw on their themes and translate them into political action. The views of the world and the prescriptions for change offered by these ideologies provide some of the main weapons which those involved in political conflicts deploy in the attempt to win popular support for their positions and programmes. For example, the Conservative party has recently attempted to convince the people of the 'commonsense truth' of the laissez-faire ideology to win support for a political programme committed to 'rolling back the state' and 'freeing market forces' from the burden of unproductive state spending. In our presentation of these ideologies, we have attempted to exemplify both these 'broader' statements of the positions and their mobilization and use by political groups and parties.

We have chosen to focus on four ideologies which recur throughout the twentieth century conflicts over welfare in Britain. These four are:

1 Laissez-faire   2 Fabianism   3 Socialism   4 Feminism

and in these units we have tried to trace their place and significance in conflicts about welfare.

We have used a rather rough and ready set of definitions to guide our choice of readings and their categorization, since real people rarely fit neatly into the boxes we design for them. The boxes we use are helpful in setting up the debates to be explored, but you should always remember that we, rather than the authors themselves, have made the decisions about where to fit them and how they relate together. Nevertheless we believe that the development of the arguments in the extracts will help you to get a real feeling for the central debates on welfare, since one or more of these ideologies has tended to dominate the discussion in all the periods we have chosen.

1.1 LAISSEZ-FAIRE

We have called this strand of ideology 'laissez-faire' because this idea refers particularly to the relationship between the state and society which its proponents have advocated — literally, that the state should 'leave alone' the workings of the social and economic aspects of society. Its propositions have however, been known by a variety of titles: in the nineteenth century as 'economic liberalism' (and in the 1970s and 1980s as 'neo-liberalism') because of its commitment to economic freedom as the basis of social order; for similar reasons it has been termed the 'free market' philosophy, while its views on the state's role have earned it the further title of 'anti-collectivism' (being against collective, social, provisions through the machinery of the state). We shall be returning to some of these difficulties in a moment, but first we want to explore some of the main elements which make up the ideology.

Its basis is in eighteenth and nineteenth century economic theory, which take the workings of market economy as the basis of the social order. Through the market (the exchange of goods and services for money), the needs and desires of the individual members of society could be brought into harmony. The economic mechanisms of the market place bring into connection the interests of the buyers and sellers of goods and services and combine all individuals in the society through a series of economic relationships. Ideally, the state's responsibility should be limited to guaranteeing the conditions of these economic freedoms. Primarily through the law, the state's task is to ensure the protection of property, the person and the contract to enable the individuals to go safely about their private business without interference. Beyond this ideal of the 'minimal' or 'night-watchman' state, the proponents of 'laissez-faire' have disagreed about what other responsibilities the state might take on in guaranteeing the conditions of economic freedom. But these disputes have always taken place within the overarching assumption that the state must not interfere with the economic freedoms of the individual. We shall be examining the nature of this relationship between economic freedom and the state in more detail in the extracts which follow, but before that it is necessary to say a few more words about the relationship between this ideology and British politics.

One reason for avoiding giving this ideology the title of 'liberalism' is that it would imply too great a connection between it and political liberalism. The relationship between laissez-faire and political parties has been much more complicated and unstable than a simple connection with liberalism would imply. It is true that during the nineteenth century laissez-faire had much of its political impact through the 'free traders' of the Liberal Party, who directed opposition to what they identified as excessive state intervention in fields of social policy introduced by Conservative governments. By the turn of the century, however, this political affiliation of 'laissez-faire' was being reversed, with the Liberal Party becoming more attached to state intervention in welfare, and the Conservative Party moving closer to defending the 'freedoms' of the laissez-faire position. Through the inter-war and post-Second World War period, laissez-faire declined in significance as a force in party political ideologies, with all the main parties moving to an acceptance of the need for state intervention in welfare (and other) fields. However, laissez-faire returned to the political stage in the mid-1970s as a key element in the 'new conservatism' of the Conservative Party led by Margaret Thatcher, which included the reassessment of laissez-faire thinkers and writers who had stood out against the post-war consensus on the expanded role of the state in social and economic life.

Even this very schematic history of the relationship between the ideology and politics indicates something of the danger of making over-simple identifications between ideologies and parties. In the extracts which follow in this and subsequent units, we shall be dealing with these problems in a more careful way in considering the 'politics of welfare' in the particular periods.

1.2 FABIANISM

We have defined the Fabian approach as one which sees the state as an instrument whose policies can be shifted on the basis of a mixture of rational argument and pressure from informed groups. Fabianism is generally characterized by the production of carefully argued reports based on detailed research. At its centre is a view of society which suggests that matters could be handled better and that the state, supported and prodded by a group of sympathetic professionals, can handle them better than the untidiness of the market. If laissez-faire ideology stands for the removal of the state — of politics — from arbitrary interference in the economy or ordinary life, Fabianism presents the contrary view that the market itself tends to be arbitrary and only the state can effectively challenge that arbitrariness as long as the functionaries of the state are sufficiently enlightened. Fabianism is the ideology of intervention to correct the operation of the free market, but the market is still expected to exist. Although many of the extracts included in the Fabian sections are by members of the Fabian Society or first appeared in Fabian publications, we are concerned with a broader tradition within which the Fabian Society played a vital, but not determining, role.

Fabians may also have a general view of the need to move towards socialism, but they overwhelmingly tend to see such a move as the product of a piecemeal series of reforms extending the role of collective (or state) provision in society based on the growth of a sector of caring and trained professionals. They have tended to be more coherent and consistent than the aggregate of official pronouncements and policy statements could ever be.

It is this which has enabled the tradition to dominate debates about social policy — at least until the 1970s. Fabians alone have been consistently arguing for a state social policy not because they were forced to make concessions to the poor nor (just) because they were appalled by the conditions of the poor, but also because their vision of the rational society is one in which the state and its experts should together make decisions for the benefit of the rest.

In the first period from which we have chosen readings, Fabianism was only beginning to develop its stranglehold over the arena of debate. The Webbs had begun to move towards the Labour movement for support and they were challenging the traditions of the 1834 Poor Law and the great Victorian charities. The voice of the rival socialisms remained strong and Fabian hegemony had not yet been achieved. By 1945 a vastly increased role for the state in providing social welfare had been widely, if not universally, accepted. The 1945-51 Labour Government seemed to confirm all the hopes of Fabianism, and on the social policy

Beatrice and Sidney Webb: leaders of the Fabian attack on the Poor Law

front the proposals of Beveridge, albeit coming from a Liberal, were accepted almost uncritically by the socialists — despite some attempts to increase benefits.

For much of the post-war period, the ideological stage was dominated by this interpretation of 1945. The main thrust, both of committed Fabians and socialists, was to highlight the erosion of the gains of 1945-51. Article after article highlighted ways in which the original criteria of need were being subordinated to market methods and argued that the universality of provision introduced after the war was being eroded by the increased use of means tested benefits.

The 1970s, however, saw a splintering of this broad consensus. It was no longer clear just how the welfare state could be maintained; nor had the post-war experience been quite as unproblematic as many on the left had implied. Not only was economic decline encouraging the employed to resist the loss of any more of their apparently declining income to the poor, but those who were the 'clients' of social services departments or having to claim benefits from the DHSS were also none too enamoured of a system which apparently required their constant supervision to prove that they were not the 'scroungers' of recurrent myth. Since a growth of welfare budgets had traditionally been based on the possibility of economic growth, the economic decline of the 1970s saw governments of both parties begin to emphasize the need to cut back and to 'live within our means'. The election of the Thatcher Government in 1979 was only the confirmation of political and ideological trends begun earlier in the decade.

In this context, therefore, Fabian ideological dominance faded. Indeed, as a clear and unified trend Fabian approaches are now far more difficult to identify — are they represented by the ex-Fabians now in the SDP, such as Peter Hall, Shirley Williams or by the now apparently very radical writings of Peter Townsend or even Michael Meacher? We shall be examining this issue in Unit 4.

1.3 SOCIALISM

Like feminism, socialism has provided its own critical commentary on the development of the welfare state, but this relationship of criticism has also made socialism difficult to identify as a separate ideology of social welfare. It has never been dominant and its attitude to the development of a social policy has always been ambivalent. After all, if many of the reasons for the existence of social problems are related to the material conditions under capitalism, surely the only social policy we really need is the social revolution? If a central aspect of the welfare state is its role as agency of social control over the poor, how can socialists make sense of alternative social policy?

Their attitude to social policy has tended to be less unified and probably less coherent than that of the Fabians. They have fundamentally been critical, pointing out the dangers of easy acceptance of or support for state initiatives and not trusting policies which do not alter or challenge the basic structures of capitalist society. They put more emphasis on the need for a new (socialist) society and on the process of class conflict or conflict between other social groups. To a large extent, therefore, they have been far more reactive to proposals, policies and events than the Fabians and their views often present an important counterpoint to those of the Fabians. At times the possibility of a socialist social policy is hinted at, at others emphasis is placed on criticism of the nature of existing policies, and at others more or less explicit programmes are put forward.

In the wake of the collapse of Fabian dominance there has been a positive explosion of debate among the more explicitly socialist writers, both about the existing and past faults of the welfare state and about possible alternatives. They have also increasingly incorporated much of the argument from the feminist tradition. Much of this debate is relatively underdeveloped, but it is already appropriate to ask whether it is from these sources that a new Fabian-type orthodoxy may arise.

1.4 FEMINISM

Although we can easily define a feminist as a woman who is fighting to improve the social, legal and economic position of all women in society it will soon become apparent as you move from one historical period to another, that exactly what this might entail has varied considerably with time. It is also important to realise at the start that at any one time not all feminists shared or share the same views on what sort of welfare policies most benefit women. Of course in any political tendency or party, members will not always agree on all policies, although they will broadly agree on political philosophy. These differences of opinion have always been particularly noticeable within feminism precisely because it has never been a political party and feminism is not a political position in the traditional sense.

Two major differences between early and modern feminism can be identified. First, although by no means all modern feminists are also socialists it is possible to identify a discernible shift to the left in feminist politics in the last 80 years. Whilst many of the suffragettes were certainly militant in their tactics (e.g. Mrs Pankhurst) their goals were often limited to the demand that women should be allowed into the public domain of politics and work on the same terms as men. They did not want to change the system, so much as to join it and to ameliorate its worst excesses. Modern feminists are more inclined to reject this approach and to demand more fundamental changes to the social order such as the abolition of the family or the introduction of wages for housework. There certainly are some feminists today who are only concerned that women should be allowed to achieve the same as men within a capitalist society, but the Women's Movement *as a whole* is now more radical than this.

A second difference lies in attitudes to organization. The suffragettes in the early twentieth century organized themselves into unions and societies such as the National Union of Women's Suffrage Societies (NUWSS) or the Women's Freedom League (WFL). These were mainly campaigning organizations which acted as pressure groups, trying to influence important members of parliament, giving public speeches and arranging public events. They were organized bureaucratically with identifiable leaders. Modern feminism has been more of a grass roots movement which has rejected leaders and bureaucratic organizations and which has attacked political institutions from outside rather than within. As you will see this has had consequences for the way in which feminists have tried to achieve policy changes.

But there are also very important threads which join the feminists of different periods together. In spite of the major distinctions that exist between early and later feminists, one crucial feature that they all shared was their emphasis on the family and marriage as a primary site of women's exploitation and oppression. Feminists have never been content with the idea that women's poverty and exploitation was simply a manifestation of class oppression. They have recognised that within the family a woman can suffer greater poverty and hardship than her husband or children and have also identified the person with whom the woman is supposed to be most intimate as the source of many of her hardships, viz. her husband (not her employer). Feminism's most vital contribution to the field of social policy therefore has been to identify women as a *special* category who need *special* benefits and provisions such as child allowances and nurseries, precisely because they suffer a double exploitation, that of poverty and class oppression and that of exploitation in the private sphere of the family. Since the turn of the century it has been the task of many feminists to criticize new social welfare policies on the grounds of their failure to take account of the special nature of women's oppression.

Throughout all of the three periods we have selected feminists have been mainly opposed to state intervention in the lives of women because this intervention has, in the main, been identified as a form of control or an unpleasant manifestation of paternalism. However what is understood by intervention has changed, so whilst modern feminists may reject state intervention in the form of DHSS special investigators or compulsory hospitalization for women giving birth, they do not reject state provision in the form of child benefits and pensions, especially where such state benefits allow women to be financially independent of their husbands or other men. Early feminists, however, sometimes took intervention and provision as being equally dangerous and feared, as did many Conservatives, that this would undermine the family and hence endanger women's economic survival. By and large however, feminists have looked to the state to provide — whether in the form of crêches or cash benefits, whilst simultaneously being cautious about the nature of that provision and wary of its possible hidden consequences for women.

1.5 CHANGE, CONTINUITY AND CONFLICT

We have chosen to present and examine these four ideologies *historically,* but in a very particular way. In Unit 1, John Clarke identified three main periods of welfare change and conflict: the 'turn of the century' (1880-1920); the end of the Second World War; and the late 1970s/early 1980s. As was pointed out there, these are only very roughly defined 'periods', for welfare history does not fit neatly into tightly defined packages of years. Nevertheless, they are useful for identifying periods of particular intensity in ideological conflicts over the nature and future of welfare. In these units, we have followed this periodization in the presentation of our ideologies of welfare. Unit 2 deals with the turn of the century conflicts; Unit 3 with the 'Beveridge Revolution' at the end of the Second World War, and Unit 4 with the late 1970s/1980s period. This way of ordering our material enables us to deal with two issues about these ideologies:

1   change and continuity; and

2   conflicts.

It is important to remember, when studying these units, that ideologies are never fixed and unchanging. The ideologies dealt with here have their own histories: they change and adapt to changing economic, social and political circumstances. In preparing the notes which accompany these ideologies, we have tried to draw your attention to continuities of themes and concerns in an ideology, as well as to where significant changes take place. It will be important to note these changes where they occur, because such changes reflect not only political developments in those who hold that ideology, but also changes in the sorts of welfare provision that are being argued about. Individuals and groups involved in conflicts about welfare in the 1980s have to take a very different set of welfare provisions as their starting point from the debates of the turn of the century.

Our second reason for dealing with these ideologies in particular historical periods is a rather different one. We want to stress that these ideologies are not merely of interest in terms of what each one has to say about welfare, but because they are *locked together* in a conflict over welfare. As you will see, many of the extracts address what they identify as the 'errors' of other positions. These ideologies are not 'competing visions' of welfare in an abstract or academic way, they are jointed in a very real competition to define and control the future direction of welfare. These ideologies are the powerful voices through which the politics of welfare is discussed for the people of the time.

1.6 READING IDEOLOGIES

In producing these units we have had to resist a common temptation for academics. In dealing with subjects like this, it is very easy to offer our version of what these ideologies say — to give our interpretation of laissez-faire or socialism. In some ways, it is easier — we read them, and then tell you what they said. But this way of presenting divergent views contains difficulties — our interpretation always comes between you and the original authors. To avoid this, we have chosen the rather more difficult path of trying to present the views of these ideologies 'in their own words'. Of course, to some extent our views still play a part. We have made the selections and have presented them in a particular way — but we have tried to keep open your access to what the authors said themselves to enable you to form your own understanding of them.

We said that it was a 'rather more difficult' way to approach the subject, and there are two sorts of difficulties involved. One is the difficulty for us in producing it, selecting extracts, explaining their context and so on. From your point of view this is less important than the second difficulty of having to read and analyse the extracts for yourselves (rather than relying on our word about what they said).

To help with this we have tried to organize our selection of extracts around a series of topics to which we think all ideologies of welfare address themselves. In this sense, our interests in these ideologies is in the different views they provide about these topics. The topics are not unfamiliar ones. You have already encountered them in your work on Unit 1. There, John Clarke used them as ways of distinguishing different ideologies in contemporary politics of welfare. Our list of key topics is as follows:

1   What is the ideology's view of existing welfare provision?

2   What does the ideology see as the effects of welfare provision?

3   What does the ideology identify as creating the need for welfare provision?

4   What welfare services does the ideology argue *should* be provided?

5   According to the ideology, *how* should welfare be provided?

6   What does the ideology see as the position of the family in the provision of welfare?

We think that these six questions provide a sort of agenda to which these competing ideologies address themselves, and our choice of extracts has been made, in part, on the basis of providing answers to them. As you work through these units, you will find that each substantial extract is accompanied by a brief exercise asking you to answer questions in relation to the example. It is worth noting down your understanding of the extract, because the final section of each unit is given over to a comparison of the different ideologies. You will find your earlier answers useful at this point.

1.7 SOME CAUTIONARY WORDS

By choosing to focus on four ideologies in this way, we run into the danger of oversimplifying. We are sufficiently convinced of the importance of these ideologies in shaping the politics of welfare in Britain to think these risks are worth taking, but we want to draw attention to some of the problems before going on.

First, in singling out these four positions for such detailed attention, we have over-simplified the ideological conflicts over welfare in Britain. People and groups have taken part in these controversies without 'belonging to' any one of the positions we have identified. They do not 'stand outside' ideology, but may, for example, draw on more than one of the ideologies mentioned here (for at various points they do overlap). Alternatively, their arguments may draw on other ideological traditions which we have not dealt with. An Open University unit is not yet capable of containing the whole realm of ideologies available in British society — fortunately!

Secondly, as we noted above, these ideological traditions are not 'pure' or self contained. In places they overlap and share arguments in common — or the same individuals may draw on more than one in constructing their arguments. We believe that there are sufficient points of difference and divergence to justify treating them as separate ideologies, but we do so in the knowledge that this over-simplifies some of the complexity.

Thirdly, not only do the ideologies change over time, but at any one time, there may be slightly differing views within the broad outlines of the ideology. This should come as no surprise: our everyday view of politics recognizes different factions of the Labour Party, and 'wet' and 'dry' Conservatives. In our extracts, too, it is possible to identify differences of emphasis and policy which can nevertheless be understood as part of the wider ideological standpoint.

And finally, a warning that ideologies of welfare are not the same as welfare policies. Policies may bear the marks of a political ideology which helped to create it — but they are rarely the direct product of such an ideology. The processes by which policies are made and enacted contain (as you saw in Unit 1) many more levels of conflict and competing demands than just those of political ideologies. We have chosen to focus on this level not because it exhausts the analysis of welfare, but because these ideologies have dominated the political and public controversies surrounding the development of the welfare state in Britain. They have been (and remain) the main 'voices' through and about which the future of welfare is argued. By the end of Unit 4, we hope you will feel that this attention has been justified.

2 THE BIRTH OF THE WELFARE STATE (1900-1914)

The early years of the twentieth century saw the introduction of a plethora of new welfare legislation and the beginnings of the legislative end of the Poor Law, although in name at least it survived until the end of the Second World War.

In 1906 local authorities were empowered to provide food for school children in needy districts; in 1907 medical inspection of school children was introduced; in 1908 employment of children outside school hours was regulated; in the same year non-contributory old-age pensions were introduced for the first time; in 1909 labour exchanges were set up for the first time; in the same year local authorities were given the power to demolish slums and insanitary houses and to build new houses; finally in 1911 the National Insurance Act was passed which, although it effectively paid for the needs of the workless from the contributions of healthy and employed workers, nevertheless set an important precedent in accepting that these groups should receive any income by right rather than as a contribution from charity. This was a period in which many of the major issues which help to determine the structure of Britain's welfare state were discussed for the first time. One of the most important manifestations of this in the years before the First World War was the argument centred on the Royal Commission on the Poor Law which reported in 1909, and extracts from which appear in more than one of the following sections.

2.1 LAISSEZ-FAIRE

By the end of the nineteenth century, the high tide of laissez-faire ideology was beginning to recede — its dominance of British economic, social and political thinking was under challenge from a number of directions. It is the growth of these challenges that make this period particularly interesting for the study of ideological conflicts about welfare and the state. Where once, laissez-faire could be (and was) presented as the 'natural order of things', a statement about the obvious truth of the working of Britain's social order, its proponents were now engaged in a more bitter conflict to maintain the position of 'laissez-faire'. In the extracts which follow, it is possible to see some of the contours of this conflict. The extracts are not merely expounding the claims of laissez-faire as a guide to social action, they are also directed at identifying the errors and dangers of other views.

Although the opposition to laissez-faire came from a variety of political positions, the defenders of laissez-faire tended to group them together under a number of labels: collectivism, radicalism and socialism. These identifying labels derived from two causes. First, as far as laissez-faire thinkers were concerned, what united these different alternatives was more significant than their political differences — and what united them was some commitment to increasing the role and powers of the state. Secondly, this 'labelling' of the other positions — particularly as *socialist* — was a central political tactic, providing a rallying cry for the defence of the existing economic and social order by creating a fear of socialism.

In the early years of the twentieth century, a variety of organizations were created to propagandize for the preservation of the 'freedoms' of laissez-faire, and to organize political lobbying against legislation for new state powers. Their origins lay in the 1880s, with the foundations of groups such as the State Resistance Society, and its successor, the Liberty and Property Defence League. In addition, a whole number of organizations directed at more specific issues and groups had developed by the turn of the century: the British Constitution Association, the London Municipal Society (to fight the growth of 'municipal socialism'), the Industrial Freedom League, the Middle Classes Defence League, and the National Free Labour Association (to protect workers against 'socialistic' trade union leaders). Many of these groups were to affiliate to an umbrella organization formed in 1905: the Anti-Socialist Union, dedicated to coordinating the struggle against socialism.

One key theme in the defence of laissez-faire was the reassertion of the 'freedom' of property against claims by 'radicals' about the duties which the propertied owed to the poor. In this first extract (written in 1879), George Jacob Holyoake provided a terse response about duties and responsibilities.

The better sort of 'Saviours' have invented seductive phrases which have heretofore beguiled me into expressions of admiration, until more discernment taught me to distrust their tendency. One was that 'Property has its duties as well as its rights.' Property, honestly come by, is for security, pleasure, and power. It has no obligations save those dictated by its interests. All men have a right to an equitable chance of property for the ends of protection and enjoyment; and in a justly organized society there ought not to exist either the necessity or duty of parting with it, when rightly obtained. When something is required to be done for those who have no means of doing it for themselves, the richer people are now expected to assist in providing what is wanted. What is this but a humanitarian confiscation of the property of those from whom such help is exacted? What is this but industrial mendicancy on the part of those who receive it? Why should workmen stoop to this? Why should they not possess the means to provide themselves with what they need? A municipality of independence, desiring some improvement, does not beg; it assesses itself for the expenses. In the same manner, the working class anywhere needing an institution, or an advantage, should do the same — pass a levy upon themselves — not pass round the hat to their richer neighbours. Property has no intrinsic duties of charity. It is the poor who have duties, not the rich; and it is the first duty of the industrious poor not to be poor.

(Holyoake, 1879)

The idea that the poor must take responsibility for their own situation was a central theme in the nineteenth century discussion of welfare (powerfully expressed in Samuel Smiles' 'Self-help') and remained one of laissez-faire's main objections to provision by the state.

One of the central political disputes over welfare in this period was fought over the future of the Poor Law. For many proponents of laissez-faire, the principles of the 1834 Poor Law came as close as possible to defining the 'proper role' of the state in welfare provision. The Poor Law empowered locally elected Boards of Guardians to provide 'relief' from distress, either as 'indoor' relief (the workhouse) or 'outdoor' relief (money payments). Relief could only be given on the basis of 'less eligibility' (i.e. at a level less than, or in conditions worse than, the norm for paid employment). The workhouse, and the less eligibility principle, aimed to deter the 'able bodied' from applying for relief rather than finding employment. The Poor Law thus aimed at providing a minimum for cases of genuine distress, where the applicants could not reasonably support themselves. For the individualists, this system — if rigorously applied — embodied the state's full responsibility for social welfare.

The Royal Commission on the Poor Law (1904-9) emerged as a key battleground in the struggle for the future of welfare. The extracts which follow are taken from the evidence given to the Commission by Thomas Mackay. Mackay was an expert on the Poor Law, author of several books about the poor, a Poor Law Guardian himself, and a member of the Charity Organization Society. This society, which aimed to coordinate the distribution of charity on a 'systematic' basis was one of the main defenders of Poor Law principles. Mackay in his evidence to the committee advocated the rigorous enforcement of the principles.

Our first extracts touch on some of his central themes about the pauper, the Poor Law and its administration.

There is an ineradicable instinct in human nature which deprives of our highest esteem the persons who allow themselves to become a public charge. Occasionally this instinct may err, but on the whole it is just salutary, and I would deprecate the suggestion which is often made, that paupers should be allowed to maintain the franchise. This position of inferiority to which by common and inevitable consent the pauper is relegated is not inhumane.

(Royal Commission, 1909, pp. 22-3)

This 'position of inferiority' of the pauper dominated much of Mackay's evidence, directed as it was to the task of using the Poor Law to 'remove' the poor. He was committed to the mixture of the economy absorbing those who wished to work and a strict regime of deterrence for those who wished for relief. His evidence referred to his belief that some Boards of Guardians were lax in their administration of the principles (especially allowing too easy and too generous a level of outdoor relief). Consequently he proposed that the elected guardians be replaced by appointed officers (stipendiaries) who could be relied on to administer 'more efficiently'. He argued the case against elected representatives as follows:

It is, I submit, no disrespect to popular local government to say that in the multiplicity of local bodies, such things as an apathetic election, an irrelevant election, an imperfectly informed election, are possible occurrences . . . An ideal administration, it may be admitted, would result from a local electorate which had made a competent study of the subject, and which, having arrived at a right principle, appointed representatives to carry it out . . . Nothing but confusion and miscarriage can result from confiding administrative duties to bodies which may be unsympathetic and ill-informed as to the wishes of

Parliament . . . especially when such bodies have full power to set the decision of Parliament at Defiance.

(Royal Commission, 1909, p. 28)

Since outdoor relief was one of the main laxities of 'unsympathetic and ill-informed' Guardians, it is not surprising that Mackay thought that outdoor relief should be withdrawn: 'I will not conceal my opinion that except in cases of emergency . . . the best thing to do would be to abolish it altogether . . .' (Ibid., p. 228). This abolition was one part of Mackay's larger vision for the functioning of the Poor Law. For him, the test of its successful functioning was *a reduction in the numbers receiving relief.* This meant making them independent of the Poor Law — and therefore no longer paupers. Outdoor relief could be replaced by carefully supervised charitable aid — or the assistance of relatives — and then, ideally, the numbers in receipt of indoor relief could be reduced by more rigorous administration thus, by reducing the number of dependents the Poor Law would succeed in its (proper) ambition of 'dispauperization' — making the poor independent.

The Majority Report's conclusion on the future of the Poor Law laid great emphasis upon the importance of linking the reform of Poor Law with organized charitable relief. At the centre of this link stood the Charity Organization Society, founded in 1869 to prevent 'indiscriminate' charity which encouraged dependence or 'demoralisation' among the poor. The Society argued that a lack of coordination between charitable providers and a lack of supervision over those who received it imperilled the recipients and led them to rely on charity rather than their own independence. Instead, the society aimed to coordinate the provision of charity and to scrutinize applicants carefully to ensure that they would make good use of the 'gift' to restore their independence. This scrutiny became known as the attempt to distinguish between the 'deserving' and the 'undeserving' poor. Further, the society insisted that charity should be accompanied by a social worker or 'visitor', who would exercise the improving force of 'personal influence' on the moral character of the recipient.

This mixture of careful investigation into the applicant's character and circumstances, and personal supervision was called 'casework' and has been identified as an important precursor of modern social work. Thomas Mackay, as both a Poor Law Guardian and member of the COS was enthusiastic about this role of systematic charity. His ideal was that

. . . that there should be no system of Public Relief at all, and that the relief of the unfortunate should be attained by a more perfect development of the natural benevolence which is inherent in family, social and industrial relationships. With an abolition of public systems of relief, the burden to fall on this private benevolence would be much lightened by the more rapid development of the self-regarding virtue of thrift, mainly, in all probability, by the expedient of insurance in many forms. It may seem a bold assertion to make, but this consummation is not, perhaps, so far out of our reach as we generally suppose.

(Mackay, 1901)

The response from the COS to the development of state welfare legislation between 1905 and 1911 was not one of open-armed welcome. The Society feared and distrusted the extension of state provision. Our next extract is taken from a speech by the Society's President, Charles Stewart Loch in which he reviewed the position of voluntary effort in the light of new state policies.

In Charity Organisation, then, what is the field for enterprise? The position of the moment is peculiar, and affects all social enterprise alike. The entrepreneur of the day is not the responsible volunteer, who, if he fails, is thrown to the lions of criticism and forgotten, but the ultra-responsible Government, which, if its measures fail, is, nevertheless, armoured against criticism and has the financial machinery and the credit of the State behind it. The larger the field its enterprise covers, the more does it reduce the enterprise of social workers to that of assisting the Government. Voluntaryism becomes an authorised sub-service. This is the tendency of the moment, though, no doubt, besides the scope which the State affords for supplementation, there are parts of the field still unenclosed by it.

I would set out the chief Social Acts since 1900 — the Enclosure Acts of the last seven years. They are these:

The Unemployed Workmen Act, 1905.
Workmen's Compensation Act, 1906.
Education (Provision of Meals) Act, 1906.
Education (Administrative Provisions) Act, 1907: Medical Inspection of School Children.
Old Age Pensions Act, 1908 and 1911.
Children Act, 1908.
Children's School Care Committees reorganised in London, 1909.
The Labour Exchanges Act, 1909.
Juvenile (Labour) Advisory Committee, 1910.
National Insurance Act, 1911.

The Poor Law remains untouched at present, but it is already being affected by the growth of State enterprise round and about it. For the rest, this list shows, all must admit, an astonishing revolution, and indicates very clearly that the spirit of enterprise in social matters has passed from the people to the State, and the people's enterprise, as must naturally follow, becomes, as I have said, the enterprise of a sub service. What the Government has established, be it rightly or wrongly, assumes such large proportions and involves so many interests that the people, or those interested in any branch of relevant work, have, by a kind of social compulsion, to arrive at the conclusion that they must make an effort to back the Government venture and do their best to make it work well. I notice, too, with some interest, that the most recent proposals for charitable progress are, in the main, proposals to link charity or social work locally to municipal bodies and generally to Government Departments. Thus the entrepreneurs of charity are running to shelter, like creatures out in a storm. The status of a Government alliance gives them protection and a certain sense of dignity.

We make numerous and almost encyclopaedic laws, and then we fail to enforce them. Can it be wondered that social conditions alter but a little among the very poor, while we press ever for more and more legislation? State authorities are wary prosecutors. They can hardly face failure. Your volunteer is a free-lance. If he fail in a good endeavour, little harm is done. He has no prestige to lose. But when it is a State affair the very amplitude of our machinery and our responsibilities, and the very largeness of the numbers with which we have to deal, may prevent our doing even simple things that require prompt attention and firmness.

These things we have noted. State philanthropy brings large numbers of the population to its ministrations. The poor, as Mr. Mackay used to say, are not usually importunate or aggressive in the case of charitable relief. Their expectations are limited. But where there is a State fund, it is to them as the income of many multi-millionaires, and there is not the same reluctance to turn it to account. A very large number of applicants necessitates alike wide supervision and a close attention to an immense amount of detail. This again necessitates a large staff and a large extension of methods of routine; and the outcome is likely to be a large and increasing bureaucracy and a popular desire to obtain Government situations such as afflicts the people of some foreign countries. Further, as this tendency prevails, the individual with his need of special help and personal attention, is apt to become one in a queue of claimants, to get a turn of help and then pass quickly out of sight. Many seek because much is offered. There is a displacement of the general will. What was left to the general public before now comes within the duty of the State as caterer-in-chief for its citizens. Thus the individual in distress and his family may find less help and consolation where they found it before, while at the same time the offers which are made to them in the new regime of State intervention may fail to meet their real wants.

PUNCH, OR THE LONDON CHARIVARI.—November 22, 1911.

THE PITILESS PHILANTHROPIST.

Mr. Lloyd George. "NOW UNDERSTAND, I'VE BROUGHT YOU OUT TO DO YOU GOOD, AND *GOOD I WILL DO YOU*, WHETHER YOU LIKE IT OR NOT."

What, then, is our enterprise? If it be possible, to humanise the action of the State, to keep alive, in spite of it, the initiative of the people, their spontaneity of character, and their independence. To humanise, as I understand it, is to keep alive and make effectual in social life that humanity or feeling of personal kindness which preserves the common sense of a race and recognise its characteristics. It is the enemy of hasty sympathy that would do good by short cuts and forced marches. It vows to be thorough in its work, because the want of thoroughness is inhumane. For the same reason, it would not act without knowledge or without anxious scrutiny of the bye-results of action. It would be adequate in its aid, because inadequate aid is but a kind of neglect. It would face the worst conditions and would not turn aside, but make a gallant and persistent effort to alter them by direct or indirect means. The humanity that would do less is a humanity dashed with fear or faithlessness. It would hand a good tradition on, for tradition lives in the safest place, the hearts and wills of good people. It would prevent pauperism, the unsettlement, listlessness, and discontent of the pauper mind, which always creep in as responsibility is diminished and independence decreases. It would prevent institutions from crushing individuality. It would apply close tests to all schemes and mark sharply what good they produce, or what weaknesses they breed. It would let no department evade this testing. It would have a measuring-rod of results, as for so many years we used the Poor Law returns, as a test of the fall or rise of dependence. State action and legislation, tested and proven to be of an injurious nature, it would oppose whole-heartedly and, if possible, criticise out of existence, whether the people were in favour of it or not. It would be inventive to meet the hundred and one difficulties of different cases, and would use all the means of suggestion and persuasion and legal constraint that are available that it may better the conditions that are found in these cases. And it would be brave.

Our final extract is from the leaflet through which the COS advertised their services. What does it tell you about their attitude to the relief of the poor?

Charity Organization Society: Notice to persons applying for assistance

1. The Society desires to help those persons who are doing all they can to help themselves, and to whom temporary assistance is likely to prove a lasting benefit.

2. No assistance should be looked for without full information being given in order that the Committee may be able to judge:
    (1)   Whether the applicant ought to be helped by charity.
    (2)   What is the best way of helping them. . . .

3. Persons wishing to be assisted by Loans must find satisfactory security, such as that of respectable householders. . . . Loans have to be paid back by regular instalments.

4. Persons who have thrown themselves out of employment through their own fault ought not to count upon being helped by charity.

5. Persons of drunken, immoral or idle habits can not expect to be assisted unless they can satisfy the Committee that they are really trying to reform.

6. The Society does not, unless under exceptional circumstances, give or obtain help for the payment of back rent or of funeral expenses. But when help of this sort is asked for, there may be other and better ways of assisting.

7. Assistance will not, as a rule, be given in addition to a Parish Allowance.

By Order,
C.O.S.
. . . . Committee

2.2 LAISSEZ-FAIRE AND WELFARE: CONCLUSION

We can now assess what sort of answers laissez-faire provides to our key questions about welfare.

1 What is their idea of the state?

Main points: The state should not exceed minimal provision in economic and social life. Such provision should conform to the basic principles of economic and social order (e.g. the Poor Law promoting 'independence'). 'Reform' in excess of this endangers the 'natural laws' on which social order is based; promotes 'expectations' among the poor, creating dependency.

2 What do they see as the effects of existing welfare provision?

Main points: Rigorously applied Poor Law principles are acceptable where they (a) meet the needs of 'real destitution; and (b) promote independence. Provision beyond this (e.g. generous outdoor relief, new welfare legislation) is expensive, bureaucratic, insensitive to 'needs' and likely to promote dependence rather than independence.

3 What welfare should be provided?

Main points: Ideally, none at all by the state. The Poor Law provides the tolerable maximum. Welfare is best left to the individual's responsibility (and family and friends) or to systematic charity. All provision should aim to foster independence.

4 How should welfare be provided?

Main points: Ideally, support should come from the network of family and friends, backed by organized public charity. The Poor Law should form a last resort — and be firmly administered to make sure only proper destitution is dealt with.

5 What causes are seen as necessitating welfare?

Main points: This is slightly difficult. A variety of circumstances (widowhood, illness, etc.) may cause destitution. But an emphasis is placed on *moral character.* Some, the 'deserving' (those who strive to be independent) should have their needs met outside the Poor Law; while the 'undeserving' should encounter relief only in the deterrent setting of the workhouse.

6 What do they see as the relationship between welfare and the family?

Main points: The family is seen as the natural basis of society, and the primary provider of support. There should be no resort to other sources of welfare until the family's resources are exhausted.

3 FABIANISM

The turn of the century saw the start of the apparently inexorable rise of Fabianism as the orthodox theology of welfarism. The Webbs — the very essence of Fabianism — had begun their careful campaigns and used the Royal Commission on the Poor Law as a magnificent sounding board for their ideas.

Both the Minority and the Majority Reports effectively called for the end of the Poor Law of 1834 (in particular the workhouse system) but the Minority Report signed by Beatrice Webb, George Lansbury, Francis Chandler and the Rev. Prebendary H. Russell Wakefield, and mainly written by the Webbs, came to dominate the succeeding debate. Some key themes of general significance for the development of social policy run through the Webbs' arguments, some of which are summarized in the first three extracts in Section 3.1. The core of their approach is highlighted in the first extract; the 'Principle of Prevention'. The Webbs call for a system which would allow officials, generally under the control of the local authority, methodically to identify social, educational and medical problem cases and to intervene to protect or cure the individual involved, thus saving and disciplining the family into the bargain.

The strong moral tone of the Minority Report, as well as the detailed nature of its proposals should also be clear from the extracts. The underlying and unstated assumption of the report is that rational discussion based on careful research can persuade those with power in society to support sensible reforms. Thus there is no attempt to identify structural problems—that is social problems for one section of society which are in the interest of another (more powerful) section. But the Webbs views were not always so 'neutral' and even the Minority Report was used as the basis for a wider political campaign, based on the new political organizations of the working class. Rational argument itself could not always win reforms; support had to be sought from sympathetic groups which might be able to generate real pressure on the central decision makers.

The Minority Report identified three specific reasons for destitution (sickness, neglected childhood and unemployment) and argued for state intervention to correct these ills. The state with the help of various institutional reforms, could be won over to a policy capable of fighting poverty. The causes of general poverty are not explored very deeply, since the concern is to identify particular individual problems which can be solved by the application of individual remedies. It is also worth noting the emphasis on unemployment and the suggestion that one of the state's tasks must be to find jobs or training for the unemployed, since this is an argument also taken up in a later period by Beveridge (see Unit 3). No government has yet been prepared to make such guarantees.

SAQ In the last part of the extract, the Webbs respond to the issue of 'moral character'. What is the main basis of this response?

3.1 THE PRINCIPLE OF PREVENTION

English Poor Law Policy

. . . Now, the inherent vice of the vast expenditure at present incurred by our Poor Law Authorities is, to the economist, not its amount, nor its indiscriminateness, but the absence of this Principle of Prevention. Except with regard to the small minority of "indoor" or boarded-out" children, and a small proportion of the sick, it cannot be said that the Poor Law Authorities make any attempt to prevent the occurrence of destitution. It is, indeed, not their business to do so. Unlike the Local Health Authority, the Destitution Authorities can do nothing to alter the social environment which is continually producing new destitution. They can do nothing for the man who is just beginning to suffer from phthisis, but who still earns wages and is not yet destitute; though they know that, in a year or two, for lack of proper provision at the incipient stage, the man will become gradually worse, and will eventually enter the workhouse, long after the curable stage has passed, merely to die. Unlike the Local Education Authorities, the Destitution Authorities cannot reach out to prevent the neglect of children which will, in time, produce "unemployables." The whole of the action and the whole of the expenditure of the existing Boards of Guardians, and equally that of the new Public Assistance Authorities proposed in the Majority Report, must, in law, be confined to the relief of a destitution which has already occurred.

If we wish to prevent the very occurrence of destitution, and effectively cure it when it occurs, we must look to its causes. Now, deferring for the moment any question of human fallibility, or the "double dose of original sin," which most of us are apt to ascribe to those who succumb in the struggle, the investigations of this Royal Commission reveal three broad roads along one or other of which practically all paupers come to destitution, namely: (a) sickness and feeble-mindedness, howsoever caused; (b) neglected infancy and childhood, whosoever may be in fault; and (c) unemployment (including "under-employment"), by whatsoever occasioned. If we could prevent sickness and feeble-mindedness, howsoever caused, or effectually treat it when it occurs; if we could ensure that no child, whatever its parentage, went without what we may call the National Minimum of nurture and training; and if we could provide that no able-bodied person was left to suffer from long-continued or chronic unemployment, we should prevent at least nine-tenths of the destitution that now costs the Poor Law Authorities of the United Kingdom nearly twenty millions per annum. The proposal of the Minority Report to break up the Poor Law, and to transfer its several services to the Local Education, Health, Lunacy, and Pension Authorities, and to a National Authority for the able-bodied, is to hand over the task of treating curatively the several sections of the destitute to *Authorities charged with the prevention of the several causes of destitution* from which those sections are suffering. This means a systematic attempt to arrest each of the principal causes of eventual destitution at the very outset, in the most incipient stage of its attack, which is always an attack of an individual human being, not of the family as a whole . . . Hence it is vital that the Local Health Authority should be empowered and required to search out and ensure proper treatment for the incipient stages of all diseases. It is vital that the Lunacy Authority should be empowered and required to search out and ensure proper care and control for all persons certifiable as mentally defective, long before the family to which they belong is reduced to destitution. It is vital that the Local Education Authority should be empowered and required to search out and ensure, quite irrespective of the family's destitution, whatever Parliament may prescribe as the National Minimum of nurture and training for all children, the neglect of which will otherwise bring these children, when they grow up, themselves to a state of destitution. It is becoming no less clear that some Authority — the Minority Commissioners say a National Authority — must register and deal with the man who is unemployed, long before extended unemployment has demoralised him and reduced his family to destitution. It is important to put the issue quite clearly before the public. The systematic campaign for the prevention of the occurrence of destitution, that the Minority Commissioners propose that the community should undertake by grappling with its principal causes at the incipient stages, *when they are just beginning to affect one or other members of a family only,* long before the family as a whole has sunk into the morass of destitution, involves treating the individual member who is affected, in respect of the cause of his complaint, even before he is "disabled" or in pecuniary distress. It means a systematic searching out of incipient cases, just as the Medical Officer of Health searches out infectious disease, or the School Attendance Officer searches out children who are not on the school roll, even before application is made. . . .

. . . Prevention is not only better, but also much cheaper, than cure. What the Minority Report asserts — and the assertion cannot fairly be judged except by reading the elaborate survey of the facts and the whole careful argument, that it has now become possible, with the application of this Principle of Prevention by the various Public Authorities already at work, for destitution, as we now know it, to be abolished and extirpated from our midst, to the extent, at least, that plague and cholera and typhus and illiteracy and the labour of little children in cotton factories have already been abolished. If this confident assertion is only partially borne out by experience, it is clear that, far from involving any increase of aggregate cost to the community, the abolition of the Poor Law and of the Poor Law Authority will have been a most economical measure.

The "Moral Factor" in the Problem of Destitution

There are those who see in this proposal to "break up" the Poor Law, ... an ignoring of what they call the "moral factor." To speak of the prevention of destitution is to such critics, equivalent to implying that all destitution is due to causes over which the individual has no control — thus putting aside the contributing causes of idleness, extravagence, drunkenness, gambling, and all sorts of irregularity of life. But this is to misconceive the position taken up by the Minority Commissioners, and to fail in appreciation of their proposals. They do not deny — indeed, what observer could possibly deny or minimise? — the extent to which the destitution of whole families is caused or aggravated by personal defects and shortcomings in one or other of their members, and most frequently in the husband and father upon whom the family maintenance normally depends.

The Minority Commissioners certainly do not ignore the fact that what has to be aimed at is not this or that improvement in material circumstances or physical comfort, but an improvement in personal character.

Two considerations may make the position clear. However large may be the part in producing destitution that we may choose to ascribe to the "moral factor" — to defects or shortcomings in the character of the unfortunate victims themselves — the fact that the investigations of the Royal Commission indicate that at least nine-tenths of all the paupers arrive at pauperism *along one or other of three roads* — the Road of Neglected Childhood, the Road of Sickness and Feeble-mindedness, and the Road of Unemployment (including "Under-employment"), must give us pause. If it can be said that it is to some defect of moral character or personal shortcoming that the sinking into destitution at the bottom of the road is, in a final analysis, more correctly to be ascribed — though on this point which among us is qualified to be a judge? — it is abundantly clear that the assumed defect or shortcoming manifests itself in, or at least is accompanied by, either child-neglect, sickness, feeble-mindedness, or unemployment. These are the roads by which the future pauper travels. Moreover, if these outward and visible signs of the inward and spiritual shortcomings are sometimes caused by these latter, it is at least equally true that the defects of character are aggravated and confirmed by their evil accompaniments.

It is by dealing with the individual through these manifestations or accompaniments of his inward defect, that we can most successfully bring to bear our curative and restorative influences. What is certain is that if we could put an end to neglected infancy, neglected childhood, and neglected youth, by whomsoever occasioned; if we could prevent all preventable sickness and infirmity, however caused; if we could either ameliorate or segregate the feeble-minded; if we could make impossible any long-continued unemployment and any chronic "under-employment," whatever its origin, we should have prevented the occurrence of nine-tenths of the destitution that is now annually created.

(Webb and Webb, 1910, pp. 299-307)

In addressing the 'moral factor', the Webbs marshal evidence about other factors creating 'nine-tenths' of destitution for which they claim priority. As the next extract indicates, they argue that welfare intervention can create the social and environmental conditions in which moral virtues would flourish.

Increase of parental responsibility

. . . The working-class woman is as devoted to her children as any other mother. But it is one of the dire results of the poverty of the poor, manifested in overwork and wages insufficient for family requirements, especially in the conditions of overcrowding and dirt imposed by residence in the slums of great cities, that the standard of cleanliness, of clothing and generally of the watchful care required for healthy childhood, almost inevitably declines. In the ignorance and listlessness, and absence of standards, which characterise whole sections of slum-dwelling families, there was in the past, and but for influence of the elementary school there would be again to-day, the very minimum of fulfilment of parental responsibility. It is the watchful influence by inspection and visitation, advice and instruction, brought to bear on the mother of the children from infancy to school-leaving age that evokes the sense of responsibility, guides and assists its fulfilment, imposes continually the higher obligations of rising standards, and has, in fact, already resulted, as all evidence proves, in the working-class mothers of the present day devoting much more time and personal labour to cleansing, clothing and generally caring for their offspring than was given, in literally hundreds of thousands of cases, by the working-class mothers of the English industrial towns and the slum quarters of the Metropolis a century ago. . . .

. . . The community cannot permanently continue to allow tens of thousands of its children to be . . . physically and mentally damaged, whether the immediate cause be poverty or cruelty, many of them inevitably graduating into crime and its accompanying dissoluteness and destitution — even if the necessary Framework of Prevention proves to be a more drastic application of the law requiring the removal of children from parents who show themselves incapable of giving to children what is understood by parental care. . . .

(Webb and Webb, 1910, pp. 613-14)

3.2 LOCAL STRUGGLES FOR WELFARE

While the Webbs (and Lansbury) were using the Minority Report to outline proposals for the overhaul of the Poor Law system, increasing numbers of Labour candidates were being elected as Poor Law Guardians. Had some of the Webbs proposals been implemented (as Quelch argues in a later extract) much of this work would have gone to higher levels or more general bodies. For the present, however, people such as Lansbury had to operate the system. Whilst some of his activities and those of his colleagues in Poplar might have found approval in the eyes of the Webbs, since they provided evidence that the machinery of local government could be used to carry out reforms, the Guardians did not operate the sort of detailed social control suggested by the Webbs. Their analysis of the causes of poverty was less systematic than that of the Webbs and focused more on immediate difficulties. The practical attempts to operate the system not only resulted in some policies which sound rather unusual by present standards (e.g. the creation of rural colonies), but also led to major conflicts with higher state agencies which aimed to resist the imposition of financial burdens on employers. The Poor Law as it existed made it possible to tax local employers through the rates and to use those funds to provide assistance to the poor, so the conflicts between different class interests became quite clear. Lansbury and his colleagues were trying to translate a general commitment to broadly socialist reforms into practice, within an existing set of local government institutions.

The extract from Lansbury sums up some of the policies adopted and fought for in this early period. Unlike the Webbs, Lansbury explicitly absolves the poor from any blame for their condition and identifies them

George Lansbury: the struggle to humanize the Poor Law

as part of the local working class. It is worth noting in Lansbury's piece the contrast with the general tone of the Webbs. There is far less of an attempt to impose moral standards on the poor, although much of the discussion of labour colonies indicates one way in which Lansbury (and others) felt standards could be raised.

SAQ When reading this extract, try to identify what Lansbury has to say about the poor and about how their needs should be met.

. . . A great part of my life has been given to the work of a Guardian of the Poor and local Town and Borough Councillor. I was first elected in 1892, when I was thirty three years of age. . . . From the first moment I determined to fight for one policy only, and that was decent treatment for the poor outside the workhouse, and hang the rates! This sort of saying brings censure on me and on the movement: it cannot be helped. My view of life places money, property, and privilege on a much lower scale than human life. I am quite aware some people are bad and deceitful. I know this because I know myself. I know people drink, gamble, and are often lazy. I also know that taken in the mass the poor are as decent as any other class, and so when I stood as a Guardian I took as my policy that no widow or orphan, no sick, infirm, or aged person should lack proper provision of the needs of life, and able-bodied people should get work or maintenance. To-day everybody agrees with this policy. I also determined to humanize Poor Law administration: I never could see any difference between outdoor relief and a state pension, or between the pension of a widowed queen and outdoor relief for the wife or mother of a worker. The nonsense about the disgrace of the Poor Law I fought against till at least in London we killed it for good and all . . .

. . . My first visit to the workhouse was a memorable one. Going down the narrow lane, ringing the bell, waiting while an official with a not too pleasant face looked through a grating to see who was there, and hearing his unpleasant voice — of course, he did not know me — made it easy for me to understand why the poor dreaded and hated these places, and made me in a flash realize how all these prison or bastille sort of surroundings were organized for the purpose of making self-respecting, decent people endure any suffering rather than enter. It was not necessary to write up the words "Abandon hope all ye who enter here." Officials, receiving ward, hard forms, whitewashed walls, keys dangling at the waist of those who spoke to you, huge books for name, history, etc., searching, and then being stripped and bathed in a communal tub, and the final crowning indignity of being dressed in clothes which had been worn by lots of other people, hideous to look at, ill-fitting and coarse — everything possible was done to inflict mental and moral degradation.

During my period as a Poor Law Guardian I was appointed a member of the Royal Commission on the Poor Laws and Relief of Distress. This was in December 1905. I received this appointment without any influence being used on my behalf, either by myself or anyone else. It came as a bolt from the blue when I received the letter from Mr. Walter Long asking if I would serve . . .

. . . This Commission published its report in 1909; there was a majority and a minority report. The minority report was the work of Beatrice and Sidney Webb, and was signed by myself, Mrs. Webb, Mr. Chandler, and Bishop Wakefield. I have never pretended to agree with every detail contained in the minority report, but broadly speaking all of us who signed agreed with its main principles. We were unanimous that the present system had outgrown whatever usefulness it had ever possessed, and that the overlapping between the Poor Law and Public Health services should be got rid of, and so we plumped straight for the abolition of Boards of Guardians, workhouses, and all such institutions. We desired that the work of Boards of Guardians should be undertaken by town, county, and urban authorities doing similar work — that is, children of school age should be under the control of education authorities, all sick persons suffering from any sickness should be cared for by the public health authority, able-bodied unemployed men and women by a national authority. There were, of course, many other details, but these were the broad principles, laying stress, of course, on the word "prevention" rather than "curative."

The years spent on this Commission were amongst the best I have spent so far as local government is concerned, because almost every moment was one spent in gathering information and knowledge concerning administration. . . . But at the end, although I still remained a Guardian and local government worker, and in a way retained my faith in parliamentary action, I came from the Commission a more convinced Socialist than when I started. My conviction grows stronger as the years pass that everything we do on palliative lines leaves some evil behind it, and that there is no remedy for poverty and destitution except the total and complete abolition of the causes which produce these evils, and that in the main, though there are many individual exceptions, these evils are social and not personal; that drunkenness and other crimes of that sort are incidental, and not of themselves the primary causes which bring about destitution most people deplore . . .

(Lansbury, 1928, pp. 129, 133, 135-6, 138-9, 142-3, 145, 146-7, 152-4, 169)

The way in which the Poplar Guardians acted on these policies set out by Lansbury involved them in considerable political controversy. Their actions far exceeded the minimal provision identified by laissez-faire thinkers like Thomas Mackay.

This question is not as easy as it may appear. At one level it is simple enough. The Webbs, argued for a 'principle of prevention' rather than one of cure. In other words social problems (like diseases) should be identified early and dealt with at that stage. Thus the Webbs' arguments provide the basis for a profession (or series of professions) whose task it is to identify these problems, and possibly also to provide sound individual preventative medicine. But the principles are not always so clear. Lansbury, for example, (and this element is also to be found in the Minority Report itself) emphasizes rather the need to combat poverty; to avoid blaming the poor and instead provide adequate resources for them. Similarly the Webbs highlight the problems of unemployment and suggest that until it is solved, poverty and the problems associated with it will continue.

The Fabians not only argue for better provision and more detailed family or household based supervision, but also have in support a set of carefully developed disciplinary procedures. If the poor or others in need of assistance do not respond appropriately, then special homes or labour colonies will be used.

All of these involve demands to expand both the responsibilities and powers of the state for greater social intervention. The Fabians argued that the 'minimal' relief offered by the Poor Law was an ineffectual and, for Lansbury, humiliating attempt to deal with unemployment and poverty.

4 SOCIALISM

4.1 UTOPIAN ALTERNATIVES

Until the rise of Fabianism and of the hard headed realists of the Labour Representation Committee in the first decade of the twentieth century, the debates of the socialists were rather more dramatic affairs. For them poverty (destitution) was simply one of more unpleasant consequences of the capitalist system and the class structure created by it. They were worried about any involvement with the capitalist state, feared incorporation and often emphasized the need to destroy that state and construct a new one. It was in reaction to these socialists that the Webbs constructed their own calculus with its detailed research, careful proposals and its ultimate reliance on benevolent administrators. In the first extract below William Morris (ironically enough in a Fabian tract), criticizes the emphasis on reforms and new machinery for socialism via the municipalities which was central to the Fabian vision. Morris saw welfare provision as a mere palliative intended to buy off those whose real interests lay in fundamentally challenging the economic system which created poverty.

SAQ Why does Morris place so much emphasis on distinguishing the *machinery* of socialism from the spirit or manner of reform?

Communism

While I think that the hope of the new-birth of society is certainly growing, and that speedily, I must confess myself puzzled about the means towards that end which are mostly looked after now; and I am doubtful if some of the measures which are pressed, mostly, I think, with all honesty of purpose, and often with much ability, would, if gained, bring us any further on the direct road to a really new-born society, the only society which can be a new birth, a society of practical equality. Not to make any mystery about it, I mean that the great mass of what most non-Socialists at least consider at present to be Socialism, seems to me nothing more than a *machinery* of Socialism. . . . Who can quarrel with the attempts to relieve the sordidness of civilized town life by the public acquirement of parks and other open spaces, planting of trees, establishment of free libraries, and the like? . . . More time might be insisted on for the education of children; and so on, and so on. In all this I freely admit a great gain, and am glad to see schemes tried which would lead to it. But great as the gain would be, the ultimate good of it, the amount of progressive force that might be in such things would, I think, depend on *how* such reforms were done; in what spirit; or rather what else was being done, while these were going on, which would make people long for equality of condition; which would give them faith in the possibility and workableness of Socialism. . . . If the sum of them should become vast and deep reaching enough to give to the useful or working classes intelligence enough to conceive of a life of equality and cooperation; courage enough to accept it and to bring the necessary skill to bear on working it; and power enough to force its acceptance on the stupid and the interested, the war of classes would speedily end in the victory of the useful class, which would then become the new Society of Equality. . . . Here again come in those doubts and the puzzlement I began by talking about . . . Whether the Society of Inequality might not accept the quasi-Socialist machinery above mentioned, and work it for the purpose of upholding that society in a somewhat shorn condition, maybe, but a safe one. That seems to me possible, and means the other side of the view: instead of the useless classes being swept away by the useful, the useless classes gaining some of the usefulness of the workers, and *so* safeguarding their privilege. The workers better treated, better organized, helping to govern themselves, but with no more pretence to equality with the rich, nor any more hope for it than they have now. But if this be possible, it will only be so on the grounds that the working people have ceased to desire real Socialism and are contented with some outward show of it joined to an increase in prosperity enough to satisfy the cravings of men who do not know what the pleasures of life might be. . . .

(William Morris, 1893, pp. 154-5)

In this extract, Morris expresses a very recurrent fear of socialists — that if piecemeal reforms take place, without a wider transformation of society, such reforms will be used merely to shore up the 'Society of Inequality'. Note that Morris is not objecting to the content of the reforms, but to the role they play in the wider social conflict.

4.2 PRACTICAL DEBATES

The debates and disagreements did not stop at this level, however. The socialist organizations continued to develop a critique of the new approaches to social policy in the first decade of the century. The Social Democratic Federation (the largest marxist organization in Britain at the time) even prepared its own submission to the Royal Commission outlining first its view that social problems (and unemployment in particular) were the result of changes in the demands of industry so that the poor themselves could not be blamed; and second presenting some alternatives, such as higher standards of provision, public works, and national farms as well as suggesting the need for an end to private ownership of production.

They took the arguments further in a debate with George Lansbury and as should be clear from the next extract prefigured some of the problems which have been identified in more recent controversies about state social policy. In particular Harry Quelch (for the SDF) argues both for more local democratic control (in opposition to the Minority Report's centralizing proposals) and against the creation of new officials and experts. He also criticizes the report for focusing on poverty as an individual rather than a social disease.

Like Morris, therefore, these socialists saw the causes of poverty in the operations of the capitalist system rather than the faults of individuals or inadequate social groups. As a result their proposals were directed against that system but, unlike Morris, they were also prepared to argue for policies which they expected to lead towards socialist change but did not, initially at least, require a complete social revolution. *Existing* welfare provision was seen as a means of policing and further harrassing the poor and the changes proposed were intended to make it possible for them to survive independently rather than under the detailed supervision of the state. They feared the growth of expert professions such as those proposed by the Webbs, emphasizing the need for locally elected councillors to be able to control the different aspects of welfare provision. The socialists paid little attention specifically to the role of the family — or of women within it — since their view was dominated by the problems of male employment or unemployment.

SAQ In reading this extract, you should consider two points. First, what do the SDF argue are the causes of poverty? Second, what do they suggest should replace the existing Poor Law?

. . . 13. Before coming to our proposals of what should be done on the abolition of the workhouses, we would impress on the members of the Commission the fact that a great deal of poverty arises from causes over which the workers as a class have no control whatever. It is no loose statement to say that over the whole field of industry such changes have taken place since 1834 as practically to revolutionise the entire system of production. The universal introduction of machinery has been a very great factor in throwing the worker out of employment, and thereby rendering him an applicant for Poor Law relief. Even where machinery has been long in use, constant improvements render a less number of human workers necessary. A great deal of machinery is automatic, and, once set going, needs scarcely any looking after. This tendency is rendering the craftsman in many industries a thing of the past; unskilled labourers — mere tenders of machinery — replace the skilled workers. This being the case, it is grim satire to see apprenticeship and the learning of a trade advocated as a step towards the solution of the unemployed question by those who should and probably do know better. The "drive" of modern industry, that is, the high pressure at which work is now carried on, also ages men more quickly, and, once their early manhood is gone, employers are not anxious to employ them. It is quite clear that this makes it harder for men and women to provide for their old age.

14. The sole object of all employers of labour, be they private individuals, or companies, or corporations of any kind, is of course to make profit. This constant casting aside of the workers, when they cease to be human profit-making machines of the highest efficiency, is a fruitful source of pauperism. The unemployed worker parts bit by bit with his home, becomes "unemployable" and inevitably drifts into the workhouse at last.

16. We may divide those coming under the Poor Law broadly into three classes: 1st, the children; 2nd, able-bodied men and women capable of earning their living by labour; 3rd, the aged, sick and infirm generally. With regard to the first and third, people of all descriptions are agreed that adequate and proper provision should be made, yet the practice has not followed this humane theory.

17. Dealing first with the children, social-democrats are of opinion that a far higher standard should be aimed at in the rearing of the children than now obtains. Schools should be built in the pure air of the country districts, the school not being one large barrack-like building, but consisting of a number of residences, each accommodating say thirty children, and each with a house-mother in charge. Meals could be taken either in the dining-room of each house, or a larger number could be grouped together. Swimming, physical exercises, music, etc., should form part of the education, and each boy and girl should be trained to some calling. Their subsequent career we will touch upon presently. The buildings should be of tasteful design and of the best material, and the food, education, and, indeed, everything in connection with the life of the children should be of the best. A sufficient amount of land should be taken in every case to provide plenty of space for playing fields and garden cultivation. The object must be to rear the youth of both sexes in the best possible way in order to produce the best possible results.

18. The aged should receive an adequate sum to live upon if they reside in their own homes or with relatives, the money being regarded as an honourable pension, and not as pauper relief. Those not able or willing so to live are to be provided for in house situated in rural districts, near enough to towns for the old people to feel that they are still in the living world, yet sufficiently far from the towns to avoid the evils of town life. Each home should accommodate a certain number of the aged, and be under the care of kind-hearted attendants. The sick should be attended at their own homes, or in excellently appointed infirmaries, and as quickly as possible sent to convalescent homes provided by the nation, the object being to restore them to robust health in the quickest and surest way. Special homes for all other infirm (epileptics, mentally deficient, deaf and dumb), should be provided nationally, and the treatment should be of a curative character.

19. The "able-bodied" are the thorn in the side of the middle-class Poor Law administrator. Yet we are convinced that inability to find employment is at the bottom of the trouble. If employment at proper remuneration were provided for all able and willing to work, the problem of the "loafer" and the "casual" would be solved, and those refusing to work, yet endeavouring to impose on others, could be dealt with. Firstly, there is scope for a large amount of employment in undertakings of national importance, such as afforestation, national main roads, reclamation of foreshores. Secondly, land could be taken over by the nation, and the men could most usefully be trained to agriculture, and to become tenants of the nation, and instead of being herded together should be paid a wage, and enabled to live with their wives and families within easy access of their work until actually becoming tenants.

20. It will thus be seen that the abolition of the workhouses could easily be brought about, and with their abolition the many evils inevitably connected with them would disappear. Other wasteful and ridiculous phases of Poor Law maladministration, such as settlement and disfranchisement, would be relegated to the limbo of the past.

21. In conclusion, as social-democrats, we want to make it perfectly clear that the problem of the Poor Law is the problem of poverty, and that poverty will be the portion of large numbers of the working class whilst the land and the wealth of the country are privately owned and industry is carried on for profit. We assert that only when the land is decreed the common property of the nation, when the wealth created by the people shall belong to the people,

and when industry is organised and controlled by the people in their collective capacity, will poverty be banished and the Poor Law or its equivalent be unnecessary. . . .

(Royal Commission, 1909)

As we suggested earlier, although identifying the causes of poverty and unemployment in the class structure and the distribution of property, the SDF do offer policies about replacing the Poor Law. These focus around the creation of decent standards (of education, pensions, alternative employment) as rights, and oppose the stigmatizing workings of the Poor Law.

4.3 SOCIALISM AND DEMOCRACY

The following extract from a debate between Harry Quelch of the SDF and George Lansbury focuses on the issue of the control and administration of welfare.

SAQ   What are Quelch's main criticisms of the Minority Report on the Poor Law?

H. Quelch, after expressing the very high esteem in which Lansbury was held by himself and the S.D.P. generally, regretted that Lansbury's name should have been appended to the Minority Report. He could quite understand that Lansbury, after his experiences on the Poplar Guardians with the ever-rising tide of poverty all around him, was heartily sick and tired of the whole business, and wanted to sweep it all away. But they did not sweep the thing away by merely changing names. There was scarcely a word that Lansbury had said in denunciation of the administration of the Poor Law with which he did not agree. But what did the Minority of the Commission propose? To abolish the directly-elected Guardians, and constitute in its place an independent bureaucratic authority; to abolish the poor rate, and have instead a parish rate; to abolish outdoor relief, but have "home aliment". They had changed the names but had not touched destitution. They could not touch destitution until they were prepared to deal with the root causes of poverty. Destitution was not a thing apart, but only a degree of poverty, which was very difficult sometimes to define. Some of the Minority proposals put forward were good, and such as Social-Democrats could support, but they had nothing to do with the fundamental changes proposed. The main proposals were anti-democratic, anti-Socialist, superficial and fallacious. They were anti-democratic because they proposed to abolish the Boards of Guardians, and every good thing that Lansbury had suggested could be carried out without abolishing them. The Guardians were the most democratically-elected body in the kingdom, and if they had not been so good as they should have been, that was the fault of the people, and their business was to educate the people to elect proper Guardians. But their administration had improved, and could improve still further. It was proposed to hand over the duties of the Guardians to the committees of the various borough councils and county councils.

What they ought to do was not to abolish the Guardians, but to abolish the pauper status. The sentiment of poor people against having recourse to the Poor Law must be broken down. He had tried to get the unemployed all to go into the workhouses, so as to force the hand of the authorities. He remembered in his young days when they had to clem and hunger day after day, week after week, because his parents would rather starve than have recourse to the Poor Law. Why did the poor resent the Poor Law? Because the bourgeois class had always so administered the law as to make it hateful and deterrent, so that people would rather die than apply for its relief. That spirit must be broken down. He did not mind the children all being under one education authority, but let it be a good education authority elected by the people for that purpose. But when they had done that, and had placed the sick under the Health Authority, the mentally defective under the Asylums Committee, the aged under the Pensions Committee, they would still need a destitution authority to deal with destitution, and to see that every person who was entitled to assistance had it. The Minority admitted that, but they wanted "a god out of the machine" — a Registrar of Public Assistance, a glorified relieving officer, representing the Central Government, and on whom they could not exert the slightest influence, and who was to be supreme. He (the speaker) had a horror of experts of all kinds. This "Registrar of Public Assistance" was to be a permanent, irremovable official; not subject to, but above, all the authorities to whose care the destitute were to be committed. His duties were thus defined:

"(i.) Keeping a Public Register of all cases in receipt of public assistance; (ii.) Assessing and recovering, according to the law of the land" — it was something to know he was not to be above the law! — "and the evidence as to sufficiency of ability to pay, whatever charges Parliament may decide to make for particular kinds of relief or treatment; and (iii.) Sanctioning the grants of Home Aliment proposed by the committees concerned with the treatment of the case."

Thus, in the last resort, it was this irresponsible official and not the local authority who would decide whether relief should or should not be granted. Yet how often, as Lansbury knew, did the relief committee of the Guardians have to override the relieving officer, and give relief against his advice!

The Minority proceeded on the assumption that destitution was an individual and not a social disease. They were merely proposing to apply curative treatment to individuals — to sort them out cheap and cure these individuals of destitution! They were not going to abolish or prevent destitution by any of these proposals. It was the bourgeoisie, the capitalist class, who were responsible for the idea of the stigma of pauperism. Destroy that idea; that was the one thing necessary to do. Whatever the form of public assistance, it was still public assistance. The great mass of the people to-day were in need of public assistance, and if the Registrar of Public Assistance were going to deal with them all he had his work cut out. By these proposals they were not abolishing Bumble, but were putting him in a higher position. It was no part of the business of the Social-Democracy to create a central authority removed from the control of the people in the locality instead of an elected body bound to give an account of its stewardship periodically . . .

. . . Parliamentary control over local matters and details was not altogether satisfactory, and could not be more democratic than a local body. He objected to the idea that Socialism meant more public officials; it did not mean a universal bureaucracy. Tramway drivers and conductors were not public officers in the useless bureaucratic sense. They must have local democratic control of the relief of destitution by a body directly elected by and responsible to the electors . . .

(Anon, 1910, pp. 4-7, 8, 9-12)

4.4 SOCIALISM: CONCLUDING QUESTIONS

SAQ What are the basic causes of poverty and destitution identified by the socialists?

In general they suggest that private ownership of the land and means of production on the basis of profit generate poverty and inequality and, in particular, they point to the changes in modern industry as creating unemployment.

SAQ What are the socialists' views of existing welfare provision?

They identify two particular failings of the existing (Poor Law) provision. First, they argue that its principles and scope are inadequate to deal with the structural problems of poverty and unemployment. Second, this inadequacy is partly represented by the Poor Law's tendency to see the causes of these problems as located in the individual. This means that Poor Law provision is not only inadequate, but also repressive and stigmatizing.

SAQ What attitude do they have to the provision of services by the state and their democratic control?

They explicitly call for particular reforms (e.g. on schools, homes for the old, etc.), but are concerned about the dangers of creating an uncontrollable bureaucracy of 'Bumbles'. This is the centre of the debate with Lansbury. They oppose notions of increased efficiency in the abstract (as suggested by the Webbs) arguing instead that since welfare is a site of conflict between classes over the distribution of resources, the greater the extent to which this is made explicit by democratic debate, the better. They reject the notion of some rational expert impartially assessing the worth of different cases.

While they put forward particular demands for welfare reforms and their democratic control, these arguments take place within the context of a commitment to change the whole social structure to remove the causes of inequality. Some socialists are suspicious of reforms which may help to maintain the structures of inequality.

5 FEMINISM

In order to understand the influence of feminism in the early years of what we now call the welfare state, it is most important to remember that prior to 1918 there were no women MPs and the majority of women did not win the right to vote in general elections until 1928. Women were therefore excluded both as policy makers and as constituents who had to be wooed to vote for particular parties. This does not mean that feminists

A feminist focal point: the struggle for the vote

had no political voice at all however but they were not central to the policy-making process. Feminists therefore acted in concert as pressure groups, and individually as moral entrepreneurs. A major function that they adopted was to expose the harshness of the majority of women's lives and to challenge the unrealistic and misguided sentimentality with which the sacredness of motherhood and wedlock was regarded.

SAQ While reading the passage from *The Mother and Social Reform* it will be valuable to keep the following issues in mind.

1 Consider how Martin accounts for the way in which women are rendered particularly vulnerable in the family.

2 How does she manage to convey the idea that women have special needs which need to be met differently to the needs of men?

3 She makes several references to the way in which income into the family might not be equally divided amongst the members of the family. What do you think this revelation might mean for policies which are aimed at the family as a unit rather than individual family members (for example the payment of maternity benefits to men)?

4 Finally what sort of provisions for wives and mothers does this extract imply are necessary? Do you think Martin is looking to the state as a potential source of material benefits for women?

The wealth of a country does not consist of its gold and silver, but of the vast complicated production and exchange of goods and services whereby the wants of the community are supplied. Unfortunately, the fact that these goods and services are usually measured against each other by means of money tends to an ignoring of goods and services not so appraised: but this does not alter their real nature. The woman's work in the home is cooking, washing, cleaning, nursing, managing is every whit as essential to society as her husband's work in bricklaying, hawking, or driving a motor-bus, and often demands greater brain power. That she should be forced into accepting degrading terms of labour, injurious to a healthy, self-respecting life, is just as deterimental to the body politic as if men were the sufferers. That the wife is in the disadvantageous position of being tied to only one possible employer should have been the most powerful of reasons for safeguarding her interests, for protecting the weaker party in the bargain. Inquiry, however, into the actual facts of the daily life of the humbler classes, as distinguished from legal fictions and conventional beliefs, reveals the truth that, as compared with the male worker, the wife suffers two fundamental disabilities: firstly, the law does not enforce contract for her as against her employer-husband; secondly, it does not, save in the feeblest and most inefficient way, protect her from his personal violence.

From one point of view marriage is merely the most important of all civil contracts. Countless unions confessedly exist where the great natural forces of love of man for woman, and of woman for man, render any idea of a hard-and-fast bargain between the parties unthinkable; where the joy of each is found in the happiness of the other, and where both willingly sacrifice themselves for their children. Nor are such unions found only among the well-to-do. But the fact that marriage in most cases has an emotional and spiritual side seems an inadequate reason for permitting the relationship in a large number of others to sink below the everyday level of business honesty and fair play. The woman takes permanent service under her husband-employer, who in return is supposed to bind himself to support her and the children she may bear, and this must be taken as meaning to support adequately. But, contrary to the general belief, the law affords her no effective redress for her employer's default.

The marriage contract is just as much violated by the husband's failure to support his family as by his misconduct, and, sentiment aside, the lack of maintenance is usually more directly hurtful to the wife and to the State.

Lord Loreburn, shortly before his resignation, in an anti-suffrage meeting declared that the English law favoured women. In the case of male workers one wonders if he would consider a contract valid, or in accordance with public policy, by which one party was held to the rendering of services payment for which on the part of the other optional. This is no small or unimportant matter. Nine-tenths of our social problems and difficulties originate in those families in which the male head of the household, either willingly or unwillingly, takes advantage of his option.

It is true that the husband is equally without legal power of compelling his wife to perform her share of the matrimonial bargain. Theoretically, this is also a serious defect in the law, but practically, does not lead to widespread evil. Among the poor, neglect of her domestic duties by the mother, in so far as she is physically or economically able to perform them, seldom occurs, save in cases of advanced alcholism or of feeble-mindedness. This is not because of any inherent moral superiority on her part, but because the incessant, insistent needs of the children train her unconsciously to self-control and unselfishness. Whatever part the fierce desire for food may have played in the past evolution of the race, in the case of the human mother the craving is, perforce, often relegated to a very subordinate place.

There is much vague, distressed talk nowadays concerning what is called 'the decay of parental responsibility.' It would be a great gain if the word 'parental' could be banished from the language for a few years. The term may refer to the father, the mother, or to both, and this ambiguity of meaning has afforded much welcome cover for obscure and confused thinking. As will be shown later, more is demanded from the mothers than ever before, but no one seems to realise that the state of the law is a direct inducement to the husbands to take no thought for the morrow as regards the number and the future of their children, and inevitably leads to their demanding from their wives a passive acquiescence in an unlimited maternity. As long as the father can, if he chooses, practically escape all pecuniary responsibility for his offspring, it is futile for eugenists and philanthropists to bewail that 'the fertility of the socially unfit is alarming and that the procreation of their kind is their only industry.' The children of alcoholic fathers, and of crushed, degraded mothers are curiously often 'well-born,' but their constitutions are rapidly undermined by their environment, and they either succumb altogether or develop serious physical defects.

(Martin, 1913)

Anna Martin's argument rests on an identification of two different conditions of work. Work in the house (women's work) lacks some of the protections which accompany waged labour — Martin identifies particularly the lack of economic independence, being bound to one 'employer' and the lack of legal protection. Martin contrasts these conditions with the demands which are made on mothers' work, which leave women responsible and allow men to be irresponsible.

Anna Martin's proposals for reform would appear to hang on the idea that the state should provide for women indirectly by enforcing men's obligations to support their wives and children adequately. Direct state provision she felt should be reserved for when the family had actually disintegrated. This position brought her into conflict with other feminists who wanted a more direct form of state support in the form of an endowment of motherhood. Martin felt this would weaken the family structure as it would reduce men's feeling of responsibility to their dependants. However it should be noted that Anna Martin was not against all forms of direct state benefits, in fact she campaigned for a better maternity grant in Lloyd George's Insurance Bill.

The National Insurance Bill of 1911 was a major impetus to early feminists to become directly involved in the development of social policy.

THE DAWN OF HOPE.

Mr. LLOYD GEORGE'S National Health Insurance Bill provides for the insurance of the Worker in case of Sickness.

Support the Liberal Government
in their policy of
SOCIAL REFORM.

By the time the bill had been drafted and debated in the Houses of Parliament the feminists had become extremely organized and well practised at lobbying. Although their main focus at this time was to campaign for the franchise they did not limit themselves to this one political goal and used their campaigning machinery on a wide range of social issues. Suffragist and suffragette journals like *Common Cause, The Vote* and *Votes for Women* all carried long discussions on Lloyd George's bill, and most of these were extremely critical of it. Only one extract is given here because most of the journals covered similar points. This one was printed in *Votes for Women* which was the weekly paper of the Women's Social and Political Union and it covers five main issues.

SAQ In reading the extract below consider the feminists' grounds for rejecting the bill. What are the main inequalities which are identified?

FIVE POINTS AGAINST THE INSURANCE BILL.

Treatment of Women under Mr. George's Proposals.

From the many fundamental defects in the National Insurance Bill as it affects women I select the following five essential points:

1. The Bill though professing to be "national," insures only four million women against sickness and none against unemployment.

As eleven million men are insured against sickness and two and half million men are insured against unemployment, and as the State is called upon to pay a contribution on behalf of each insured person, the discrimination against women is very pronounced.

This discrimination is increased by the fact that a much larger proportion of women will fail to obtain admittance to the friendly societies and will be thrown back on the Post Office scheme, which is not really insurance, but compulsory thrift.

2. Working women, who, as wives and mothers or as sisters or daughters, are giving up their lives to the care of the home are not insured under the Bill, and of the widows who are left with young children to take care of, only a very small proportion can obtain benefits under it.

Working for others in the home is penalised by exclusion from insurance, and a premium is put on earning money wages. Not only so, but every year which an unmarried girl devotes to "home duties" after she leaves school is reckoned to her disadvantage, and she gets smaller benefits when she at last becomes a wage earner and enters the scheme, while if she continues her home duties until she marries and is subsequently left a widow, she is placed at special disadvantage under the Bill.

Widows with young children will generally only be eligible for the "voluntary" side of the scheme, and as this means a weekly contribution of 6d. out of their scanty earnings will very rarely be able to become insured.

The exclusion of wives from the scheme renders the expenditure on sanatoria a farce, for what is the use of segregating male consumptives while leaving women to spread infection in the home?

3. Women get lower benefits than men for the same premium.

Mr. Lloyd George claims that where men pay 4d. premium women pay 3d. premium, so that there is no injustice in women receiving 7s. 6d. sick benefit where men receive 10s. But the difference in premium only relates to those earning *over 15s. a week*. Where the wage-earner is getting *less than 15s. a week,* and a very large number of women earn less than this amount, the premium paid by the employee is precisely the same for men and women, yet the man's sick benefit is 10s. and the woman's only 7s. 6d. (Note the amount of cash benefit is never more than two-thirds the weekly wages, but is to be made up to the full value of 10s. for men and 7s. 6d. for women by other benefits.)

4. Premiums paid in out of moneys jointly earned by husband and wife are credited solely to the man's account.

When a man and woman marry, the wife usually agrees to give up earning an independent living, and to devote her life to the care of home and children. There is thus a division of labour, the husband doing the external work and the wife the internal work; this domestic arrangement has led many people erroneously to suppose that the money paid to the husband is solely his instead of being in reality the joint product of the labour of husband and wife. The Insurance Bill follows this erroneous assumption, and in compulsorily taking a share of the family income, credits it wholly to the man's account, insuring him therewith against sickness, while leaving the wife uninsured. A particularly flagrant example is that of the wife of a small shopkeeper, who helps to build up her husband's business, and to pay his premium, and yet is debarred from benefit, either during his life or after his death.

5. Only a very small proportion of women obtain anything like a *quid pro quo* for their payments.

To understand this, it is necessary to realise that sickness does not occur equally at all ages. In the early part of life, periods of invalidity are few and short, but later they become more frequent, until at the age of sixty a considerable proportion of men and women are unable to earn their own living. From this it follows that men and women who do not live to be old do not, unless they suffer to an unusual extent from sickness, get value for all the premiums paid on their behalf. So far there is nothing particularly unjust, it is the usual principle underlying insurance. But there is this difference between men and women, that whereas the great majority of men will be insured up to the day of their death (or till they reach 70 and get the state-paid old age pension), the great majority of women will only be insured during their young years — until they marry, in fact — and of those women who live to be old only a very small proportion will be insured. They will therefore pay large premiums for small benefits in their youth, and when they are old will not reap the reward of their thrift.

Mr. Lloyd George attempts to meet this criticism by saying that the funds of men and women will be kept separate and that all the premiums paid on behalf of women will be credited to the women's account, but this answer does not meet the case, for the simple reason that during the larger part of a working woman's life her labour instead of helping her to build up her insurance fund is solely helping her husband to build up the fund against his own old age.

(Pethick Lawrence, 1911)

Pethick-Lawrence identifies five main issues about the National Insurance Bill which involve unequal treatment of women. The coverage of the proposals is itself selective; women working in the home rather than waged work receive no cover; women receive lower rates of benefit; all premiums paid are credited to the man's account; and even where women are part of the scheme they are unlikely to receive the same totals of benefits.

Because of the importance which these feminists attached to women's work in the home, and the importance of giving women some economic independence, the campaign for the Endowment of Motherhood became an issue of major significance.

5.1 THE ENDOWMENT OF MOTHERHOOD

The campaign for the endowment of motherhood relied very heavily on the evidence of the appalling health conditions endured by the working classes which had been revealed by the First World War. But it also gained great impetus by the discovery that the health and welfare of children improved during the war when mothers had the benefit of the regular Separation Allowance paid by the state to the wives of soldiers. This policy revealed that women were better able to rear children on fairly small state benefits than on their husband's housekeeping provision. The Endowment of Motherhood Society used this evidence to argue for a form of family allowance during peace time.

In the following extract written by A. Maude Royden it is possible to identify most of the principles of a feminist position on state benefits in the early twentieth century. These principles can be summarized as:

1   a rejection of the stigma of charity and an assertion that state provision for the endowment of motherhood is an *earned* benefit,

2   an insistence on practical measures and a rejection of rhetoric about the sacred role of mothering,

3   a rejection of a means tests for this type of benefit and a refusal to divide mothers according to their social class,

4   a rejection of state intervention in the form of surveillance over mothers who receive the endowment.

In practical terms the extract also reveals how the society wanted the endowment to be administered, and in strategic terms it can be seen that the feminists tried to make the scheme attractive to the trades unions and working class men. In reading the extract it is important to identify all these issues.

National Endowment of Motherhood

The war, with its terrible toll of young life, has taught us the value of babies. They used to be called "encumbrances"; now we are beginning to reckon them up as jewels. But while we dwell on the need for more young citizens to build up the new world, scold their mothers for not bearing and rearing a larger number, and hold "Baby Weeks" in order to give louder expression to our changed views as to the value of babies, we have as yet done little to lighten the burden of those who have families to support, or to create the conditions in which mothers can give the best service they are capable of, to work which is truly "of national importance."

Something is being done by the provision of schools for mothers, baby centres, district nurses, the registration of midwives, and other reforms. But the fact remains that the heads of families are still heavily penalized compared with those who have no such responsibilities; the burden on the shoulders of the working-class mother remains as heavy as ever; and the children suffer as a result.

To these vexed questions there can be no single solution. The one that comes nearest to an answer to them all is the National Endowment of Motherhood.

What exactly does this answer mean? It means that the State shall make a grant to every mother of children, *plus* an allowance for each child up to the age when it goes to school.

In such a scheme there is no taint of pauperism or philanthropy. It is a recognition of the inestimable services rendered to the State by mothers, and so long ignored. It should therefore be given not to "necessitous" mothers only, as though it were a kind of charity, but to *all*. It should be paid by some authority other than the Poor-Law Guardians and the relieving officer. It should be wholly outside the Poor Law, for it would be in no sense "relief"; it would be well earned, we know, and those who earn should not be treated as though they were objects of charity or paupers.

It will be said, "But you cannot *pay* mothers for what they do for their children." Of course you cannot. You cannot buy with all the money in the world love and devotion and the willingness to risk life itself to bring life into the world. The mother is perhaps, in one sense, like the soldier. You cannot *pay* a soldier for what he does. You cannot pay a man to be patriotic; you cannot pay him to die; you cannot pay him to give what no money can ever restore or make good to him.

But you do not, therefore, argue that he should have nothing at all. You do not say to him, "Your service is so sacred and noble that we do not dream of offering you any money. If you should happen to want any, no doubt your commanding officer will give you what he thinks proper." No; the soldier does not get much, but at least we do not leave him without *anything* in return for all he does for us.

Why, then, should mothers be treated so? Why should we say to them, "Your work is so honourable and sacred that you cannot possibly want any money, and if you should wish to give your husband a Christmas present, you will have to ask him to give you the money for it!"

Every member of her household gains in importance and feels himself of value in the world as he (or she) begins to earn even a little money. Only the mother's work receives from the world no recognition but a flood of empty talk. And if her husband dies she is left absolutely unprovided for, and expected to put her children into some charitable institution and go out to work. Someone, of course, must be paid to run the institutions and look after the children — to make, in fact, an artificial home for them. Would it not be better in every way to leave them in their real home and hand over the money they cost to the real mother to keep it up with? Enable her to do her work as she would like to do it, free from the intolerable strain of anxiety about ways and means. Let her know that, whether her husband is out of work for a while or not, incapacitated by illness or not, even if he deserts her or death bereaves her, she will still be able to keep her children with her and her home together — not indeed in such comfort as when her husband's earnings were in partnership with hers, but at least without the fear of destitution before her eyes.

It is therefore proposed that the system now in existence, of giving to the wives of soldiers a regular weekly allowance for themselves and each child — 12s. 6d. for the wife, 7s. for the first child, 5s. for the second, 3s. 6d. for the third, and 3s. for subsequent children — should be continued after the war and extended to all mothers of young children. It should not be given as a reward for special virtues, nor as a relief to the destitute, nor as a philanthropic dole; but as a recognition of a great, sacred, and essential service rendered by mothers to the race. As such it should be paid neither by the relieving officer nor by any philanthropic society, but by some agency such (e.g.) as the Ministry of Pensions, at present responsible for the payment of separation allowances.

The rate should be the same for all, and should be paid to all. Class feeling should no more be allowed to enter into this great reform than at present it enters into the payments made to soldiers. Every man who enlists receives the same pay, whether he be a duke's son or a dock labourer, and no one is snobbish enough to refuse his pay because he "does not need it." The amount spent on the rich would be a minute proportion of the whole, and much less than they would be called on to pay in taxation. It would be well spent in establishing the principle that every mother renders the same great service and every child's life is of a value which is not affected by class. Moreover, the inclusion of *all* mothers would tend to reduce the danger of compulsion and inspection to a minimum, for no one is in a hurry to inflict these things on the rich. The working classes already have only too much to suffer from inspection.

The endowment of motherhood seems therefore to have all the qualities of a really great constructive reform. The idea is as yet in its infancy: it will have to be discussed and modified by criticism and by experience till the best possible scheme is found to embody it. But we have already, in our system of separation allowances, made a beginning, and found it works well. When the war is over, will the devotion and labour of mothers be worth less to the nation than now? Or the life of a child born the day after the terms of peace are signed be of less value than that of the child born to-day? If the answer to these questions is "No," let us begin at once to work for a system under which the devotion of all mothers, the lives of all little children, shall at least be safeguarded from the worst kind of privation.

(Royden, 1918)

Eleanor Rathbone and the Endowment of Motherhood Society continually worked on the endowment plan to try to produce the best possible scheme. One of the main problems the plan faced was to find a source of

Eleanor Rathbone: campaigner for the Endowment of Motherhood

funding to cover the immense costs. Ultimately Rathbone attacked the family wage system and decided that men's wages should be reduced in order to pay for the children's allowance. In a pamphlet entitled 'Why Women's Societies should Work for Family Endowment', in 1919 Rathbone and Mary Stocks put forward the following brief plan.

Put as briefly as possible, the plan is as follows:

Let the basic minimum wage for adults be "a living wage" for two persons, determined annually according to the cost of living. This allows for the maintenance of the wife, parent, landlady, or other "home maker" of the industrial worker.

Subject to this basic minimum wage, let the actual wage paid for every grade of worker be determined as at present by the usual machinery of negotiation between employers and employed.

Provide for the children separately as follows: Let the number of children of employees in the industry or industries included in the arrangement be estimated annually; also the minimum cost of a child's maintenance.

The total sum needed having thus been ascertained, let every employer be required to pay his share of it, calculated according to the number of his adult employees, whether men or women, married or single, into a central fund called "The Children's Fund." Out of this fund, let an allowance be paid monthly on behalf of every employee's child to its mother or acting female guardian.

The advantages of this plan are:

(A) It relieves industry of the burden of attempting to pay a family wage to every man, whether he has a family or not. (It is calculated that in Australia the saving effected would be £66,000,000 per annum, as compared with the cost of paying all men on the five member family basis.)

(B) It secures to every worker and his wife or other "home maker" an income at least adequate to the needs of healthy physical subsistence.

(C) It secures that the money intended for the maintenance of the children is paid directly to the mother.

(D) It gives the employer no inducement to prefer single to married men, or women to men, or men to women, but leaves him free to select the best worker for the job.

(E) By removing the chief obstacle to "equal pay for equal work," it enables industry to make full use of the industrial capacities of women, without injustice to men.

(Rathbone and Stocks, 1919)

A major importance of the Endowment of Motherhood Scheme was the way in which it revealed that in order to do something about the economic condition of dependants in the family (the private sphere), something had to be done to rearrange the wage system in the public sphere. This was a radical insight which did not make the society at all popular with trades unions or employers who did not want wage bargaining influenced by extraneous factors like the needs of dependant women and children. But Rathbone's critics were not all located within traditional male bastions, in fact she was criticised by other feminists most notably Anna Martin.

We have already seen that Martin was reluctant to have direct state aid paid to the family and her arguments against the endowment of motherhood focused on two major issues. She suggested that it would become an economic incentive for men to father large numbers of children, so as to benefit from the income they would produce. Secondly, she argued that the removal of economic responsibilities from the father would be 'demoralizing', he would lose his incentives to work and maintain his family. Both of these effects, she suggested, would bear heavily on mothers. The first would create greater physical demands of child bearing and rearing; while the second would increase the mother's responsibilities for the family. Martin's criticisms, although from a feminist concern with the position of women, share some of the views of laissez-faire thinkers about the effects of state benefits being to undermine 'independence'.

5.2 FEMINIST ARGUMENTS

Anna Martin's criticisms of the Endowment of Motherhood indicate the diversity which can exist within these broad 'ideologies'. Her concern for greater legal protection and independence for women is connected to moral arguments about the need for constraints on the irresponsibility of male workers. By contrast, others argue for the necessity of putting women's economic independence first, and place less emphasis on the legal protection of women's rights in the family, both, however, focus on the conditions of women's work in the home as a major cause of inequality.

SAQ What do the feminists identify as the main causes of social problems?

The issues we have encountered here do not cover the same range as those in the earlier sections, but focus on those which connect to the family and women's position. The arguments focus on the inequalities involved in women's work in the home and the lack of economic and legal independence associated with it. They differ in their explanations of these inequalities, but they share this focus of concern, and point to the serious effects — for women and children — that follow from them.

SAQ How do feminists see existing welfare provision?

Each of the authors we have studied points to the failure of the state to provide adequate protection or provision for women either as workers or as mothers. The family and the society benefit from women's work, but pay little attention to it. No provision exists which would increase women's independence.

SAQ   What sort of welfare do feminists think should be provided?

We have seen that feminists had different views about what welfare provision should be created. For many, provision should be made which made the woman more independent, and thus able to fulfil her responsibilities as wife and mother from a more securely guaranteed economic basis. This was the argument which underpinned the case for the endowment of motherhood.

Others argued for the equalization of treatment under existing provision, for example in the 1911 National Insurance Act. By contrast, writers like Anna Martin feared the effects of giving direct economic aid to women, and argued instead for a stricter enforcement of the marriage 'contract' to provide greater legal protection for women.

6 CONCLUSION

The turn of the century marked a major transition in the relationship between the British state and welfare provision. As we have seen this transition developed through a major attack on the old provision (the Poor Law) and the emergence of new forms of welfare. Of the arguments we have considered in this unit, only those for laissez-faire favoured preserving the old, while the others, in very different ways, entered the conflict for new forms of welfare. Here we want to summarise the key issues around which these conflicts took place.

Laissez-faire proponents viewed the Poor Law as being a sufficient level of state provision for poverty. Its principles — particularly that of 'less eligibility' — reflected the laissez-faire view of the basis of poverty being in individual character and morality. The provision of relief through the firm application of the Poor Law and rigourously administered charity gave the means for effectively distinguishing the 'deserving' from the 'undeserving' poor. They resisted the expansion of welfare provision by the state on a number of grounds. They feared that the creation of 'rights' to welfare would undermine individual independence, and create a class of 'demoralized' state dependants. They argued that the cost of welfare would be excessive, and that welfare would be administered through cumbersome bureaucracies which would be insensitive to individual cases.

The Fabians in this period focused on attacking the Poor Law, criticizing it as an inadequate and inefficient response to the varied causes of poverty. They argued for the need to research and analyse the real facts about poverty, and that such evidence should provide the basis for rational solutions, nationally administered by trained experts. Although they did not actively support the Liberal reforms of 1906-14, believing them not to be systematic enough, their influence on the creation of those reforms (particularly unemployment insurance) was substantial.

Perhaps more importantly, the Fabians created an *ideology* of welfare provision — based on scientific research and administrative expertise — which was to become increasingly influential.

Socialists also argued that the Poor Law was inadequate, but primarily because it failed to comprehend the structural basis of poverty in the distribution of wealth. They also pointed to the moralizing and punitive character of the Poor Law. Socialists remained suspicious of further reforms, designed as they saw it, to preserve rather than change a society of inequality. Particularly, they criticized the insurance basis of welfare reform — arguing that this made the poor pay for their own benefits. Instead they argued for broader benefits which would be paid for out of redistributive taxation. Alongside this, they argued the need for the democratization of institutions providing welfare.

Finally, **Feminists** argued that welfare reforms were missing a key issue, that of the position of married women in the family. They suggested that, with such national emphasis being placed on childhood and the family, welfare reform should take the duties and responsibilities of the mother seriously. They pointed out that married women were in a vulnerable and dependant position — vulnerable to their husband's wishes and economically dependant upon his goodwill. There were differences in their proposed solutions to this dilemma, ranging from a more powerful legal enforcement of the marriage contract as a contract to the proposals for the endowment of motherhood. They were highly critical of insurance-based reforms which treated married women unequally, and thus perpetuated their position of dependance.

These, then, were the core themes of the welfare debate at the turn of the century. The welfare reforms of 1906-14 do not 'belong' to any of these ideologies, but reflect something of the conflict between them and the social groups which they represented. They recognised the pressure of working class demands to move beyond the limits of the Poor Law, but tied the new provisions to an insurance-based system. Although not finally abolishing the Poor Law, nor creating a systematic structure of welfare, the Fabian principles of sound administration and the promotion of national efficiency were embodied in the reforms. The endowment of motherhood, by contrast, was to wait a much longer time for political recognition.

REFERENCES

ANON (1910) Report of the Debate on the Poor Law Minority Report, between G. Lansbury and H. Quelch (Editor of *Justice*), London, Twentieth Century Pamphlet.

LANSBURY, G. (1928) *My Life,* London, Constable.

HOLYOAKE, G. J. (1879) 'State socialism', *Nineteenth Century,* June.

MACKAY, T. (1901) *The Public Relief of the Poor,* London, John Murray.

MARTIN, A. (1913) *The Mother and Social Reform,* reprinted in *Married women and Social Reform* — a collection of papers by A. Martin published in the journal *The Nineteenth Century.*

MORRIS, W. (1893) *Communism* Fabian Tract 113, in BRIGGS, A. (1962) *William Morris: Selected Writings and Designs,* Harmondsworth, Penguin.

PETHICK LAWRENCE, F. W. (1911) 'Five points against the Insurance Bill', *Votes for Women,* 27 October.

RATHBONE, E. AND STOCKS, M. (1919) *Why Women's Societies Should Work for Family Endowment,* a pamphlet.

ROYAL COMMISSION ON THE POOR LAW AND RELIEF OF DISTRESS (1909) Appendix to Vol. 3. Minutes of Evidence 49th — 71st days, Cmnd 4755, London, HMSO.

ROYDEN, A. M. (1918) *National Endowment of Motherhood,* a pamphlet.

WEBB, S. and WEBB, B. (1910) *English Poor Law Policy* (reprinted 1963), London, Cass.

ACKNOWLEDGEMENTS

Grateful acknowledgement is made to the following sources for material used in this unit:

Text

George Allen and Unwin for C. S. Loch, *A Great Ideal and its Champion,* 1933; The London School of Economics and Political Science for S. and B. Webb, *English Poor Laws Policy,* Longman, 1910; Constable Publishers for G. Lansbury, *My Life,* 1928; Automated Reproductions for A. Martin, 'The mother and social reform', in *The Nineteenth Century,* 1913.

Illustrations

pp. 9, 26, 37 and 42 BBC Hulton Picture Library; *p. 19 Punch,* November, 1911; *p. 34 The Graphic,* 3 November, 1906.

UNIT 3

IDEOLOGIES OF WELFARE: THE MOMENT OF '1945'

Prepared for the Course Team by Allan Cochrane, Carol Smart and John Clarke

CONTENTS

1 INTRODUCTION: THE MOMENT OF '1945'

In this unit, you will be considering some of the main arguments which surrounded the expansion of state welfare provision at the end of the Second World War. These new policies are often referred to as the 'moment of 1945' because of the way they were so deeply intertwined with the ending of the war and the return to party politics from the cross-party War Government. In planning and execution, however, the policies of the new welfare state cover a larger number of years.

Campaigning to win the peace

Many of the policies, and the arguments and beliefs which supported them had their roots in responses to the Depression of the 1930s. The wish to avoid a return to mass unemployment and all that accompanied it motivated a whole variety of politicians, parties and experts to take more seriously the prospect of an expanded role of the state in managing the economy, and in providing welfare services. These ideas were to receive a massive popular backing emerging not only from memories of the Thirties, but from the character of popular involvement in the war. This 'People's War' generated demands not only for victory *over* fascism, but a victory *for* a better society.

As Unit 1 indicated, these political and popular beliefs met in the symbol of the Beveridge Report of 1942. The idea of the 'Beveridge Revolution' came to express the social purpose of the People's War, and offered the vision of a reconstructed British society, moving away from the grossest injustices and inequalities of the past.

The political experience of the war made these reforms more possible in a number of ways. The coordination of economic planning by the government (ranging from the direction of production and labour to the 'equality of sacrifice' of rationing) made it clear that economic and social intervention by the state was a real possibility — and not just a political fiction of 'socialists' or 'collectivists'. Secondly, the involvement of employers' representatives and trade union leaders into war planning indicated the basis on which 'corporate' political and economic planning by the state could proceed after the war. Finally, the alliance with the USSR removed (temporarily at least) the ideological slur of 'communist' from the political repertoire. The Soviet Union became a valued ally receiving much political and popular support, including from such previously (and subsequently) fervent anti-communist members of the war cabinet as Lord Beaverbrook.

The Beveridge proposals on social insurance were not the only elements which made up the new post-war welfare state, even though his report was to stand as a symbol of those reforms. The legislative programme covered a whole variety of welfare innovations, including

1944 Education Act: providing secondary education for all in a tripartite system of grammar, technical and secondary modern schools.

1945 Family Allowances Act: providing universal benefits for families with two or more children.

1946 National Insurance Act: reorganizing and extending the scope of unemployment, sickness and other insured benefits.

1946 National Health Service Act: reorganizing health provision to provide universal services free at the point of delivery.

1946 Town and Country Planning Act: to provide greater central and local government powers of planning and development.

1948 Childrens Act: to provide local authority Children's Departments, staffed by social workers, with the powers to coordinate services for children in need.

1948 National Assistance Act: to reorganize the provision of uninsured benefits for those whose needs (in old age, sickness and unemployment, for example) could not be met through the National Insurance scheme.

In the arguments surveyed in this unit, we have focused on those which surrounded Beveridge, his report and the plans for social insurance and family allowances, for, just as the Beveridge Report became the public symbol of the welfare state, it was also the focal point for the arguments about the provision of welfare by the state.

2 FABIANISM AND WELFARE

Nineteen forty-five has become a symbol of the zenith of Fabianism. Although Beveridge in some ways fits rather better with a Liberal social welfare tradition, such was the all-encompassing range of his report that it seemed to come from the more programmatic Fabian tradition. He may not himself have felt that his ideas pointed towards socialist ends — even in the longer term Fabian sense — but they were certainly taken up enthusiastically both by the Fabians (see second extract by Robson) and most other socialists, as confirmation of their ideas and policies. So, for example, Jennie Lee, standing as an Independent Labour candidate in Bristol in 1943 against the coalition candidate made it clear that 'I stand for every word, every letter and comma in the Beveridge Report . . .' (quoted in Addison, 1977, p.226).

This enthusiasm may have been rather short-sighted (as we shall see later in considering more modern debates) but it is difficult to exaggerate its strength at the time. Beveridge and the ideology of Beveridge not only dominated the 1945-51 period but set the tone for many of the debates since then between different groups who seem to be squabbling over his heritage. Only in the last decade have more serious attempts been made to go beyond it. If in 1945 we all suddenly became Keynesians, we rather more obviously became Beveridgians — children of the welfare state.

The proposals contained in the Beveridge Report were intended to ensure a minimum level of subsistence on the basis of a universal national insurance system, backed by national assistance where necessary (now metamorphosed into supplementary benefit). Two points perhaps should be raised here: first, Beveridge emphasized the need for subsistence — no more. He feared that any greater payment than this might discourage people from seeking work and wanted to make sure that those out of work would not be paid more than those in employment. Second, the insurance principle on the basis of which social security was to be provided and resources to be redistributed meant that the employed could be expected to continue to pay for the unemployed albeit on a national rather than 'approved society' scale. But like the Webbs, in the earlier period, Beveridge also made it clear that one condition for the success of his scheme was that the government would aim for the maintenance of full employment. (He developed this notion in a later book: *Full Employment in a Free Society* (1944)). In the first extract given here, Beveridge places his basic proposals in a wider social policy context, as part of the programme for the post-war reconstruction of Britain.

Social Security and Social Policy

. . . 409. Social security as used in this Report means assurance of a certain income. The Plan for Social Security set out in the Report is a plan to win freedom from want by maintaining incomes. But sufficiency of income is not sufficient in itself. Freedom from want is only one of the essential freedoms of mankind. Any Plan for Social Security in the narrow sense assumes a concerted social policy in many fields, most of which it would be inappropriate to discuss in this Report. The plan proposed here involves three particular assumptions so closely related to it that brief discussion is essential for understanding of the plan itself. These are the assumptions of children's allowances, of comprehensive health and rehabilitation services, and of maintenance of employment. After these three assumptions have been examined, general questions are raised as to the practicability of taking freedom from want as an immediate post-war aim and as to the desirability of planning reconstruction of the social services even in war.

Assumption A. Children's Allowances

410. The first of three assumptions underlying the Plan for Social Security is a general scheme of children's allowance. This means that direct provision for the maintenance of dependent children will be made by payment of allowances to those responsible for the care of those children. The assumption rests on two connected arguments.

411. First it is unreasonable to seek to guarantee an income sufficient for subsistence, while earnings are interrupted by unemployment or disability, without ensuring sufficient income during earning. Social insurance should be part of a policy of a national minimum. But a national minimum for families of every size cannot in practice be secured by a wage system, which must be based on the product of a man's labour and not on the size of his family. The social surveys of Britain between the two wars show that in the first thirty years of this century real wages rose by about one-third without reducing want to insignificance, and that the want which remained was almost wholly due to two causes — interruption or loss of earning power and large families.

412. Second, it is dangerous to allow benefit during unemployment or disability to equal or exceed earnings during work. But, without allowances for children, during earning and not-earning alike, this danger cannot be avoided. It has been experienced in an appreciable number of cases under unemployment benefit and unemployment assistance in the past. The maintenance of employment — last and most important of the three assumptions of social security — will be impossible without greater fluidity of labour and other resources in the aftermath of war than has been achieved in the past. To secure this, the gap between income during earning and during interruption of earning should be as large as possible for every man. It cannot be kept large for men with large families, except either by making their benefit in unemployment and disability inadequate, or by giving allowances for children in time of earning and not-earning alike.

Assumption B. Comprehensive Health and Rehabilitation Services

. . . 426. The second of the three assumptions has two sides to it. It covers a national health service for prevention and for cure of disease and disability by medical treatment; it covers rehabilitation and fitting for employment by treatment which will be both medical and post-medical. Administratively, realisation of Assumption B on its two sides involves action both by the departments concerned with health and by the Ministry of Labour and National Service. Exactly where the line should be drawn between the responsibilities of these Departments cannot, and need not, be settled now. For the purpose of the present Report, the two sides are combined under one head, avoiding the need to distinguish accurately at this stage between medical and post-medical work. The case for regarding Assumption B as necessary for a satisfactory system of social security needs little emphasis. It is a logical corollary to the payment of high benefits in disability that determined efforts should be made by the State to reduce the number of cases for which benefit is needed. It is a logical corollary to the receipt of high benefit in disability that the individual should recognise the duty to be well and to co-operate in all steps which may lead to diagnosis of disease in early stages when it can be prevented. Disease and accidents must be paid for in any case, in lessened power of production and in idleness, if not directly by insurance benefits. One of the reasons why it is preferable to pay for disease and accident openly and directly in the form of insurance benefits, rather than indirectly, is that this emphasises the cost and should give a stimulus to prevention. As to the methods of realising Assumption B, the main problems naturally arise under the first head of medical treatment. Rehabilitation is a new field of remedial activity with great possibilities, but requiring expenditure of a different order of magnitude from that involved in the medical treatment of the nation.

427.   The first part of Assumption B is that a comprehensive national health service will ensure that for every citizen there is available whatever medical treatment he requires, in whatever form he requires it, domiciliary or institutional, general, specialist or consultant, and will ensure also the provision of dental, ophthalmic and surgical appliances, nursing and midwifery and rehabilitation after accidents . . .

Assumption C.   Maintenance of Employment

. . . 440.   There are five reasons for saying that a satisfactory scheme of social insurance assumes the maintenance of employment and the prevention of mass unemployment. Three reasons are concerned with the details of social insurance; the fourth and most important is concerned with its principle; the fifth is concerned with the possibility of meeting its cost.

First, payment of unconditional cash benefits as of right during unemployment is satisfactory provision only for short periods of unemployment; after that, complete idleness even on an income demoralises. The proposal of the Report accordingly is to make unemployment benefit after a certain period conditional upon attendance at a work or training centre. But this proposal is impracticable, if it has to be applied to men by the million or the hundred thousand.

Second, the only satisfactory test of unemployment is an offer of work. This test breaks down in mass unemployment and makes necessary recourse to elaborate contribution conditions, and such devices as the Anomalies Regulations, all of which should be avoided in a satisfactory scheme of unemployment insurance.

Third, the state of the labour market has a direct bearing on rehabilitation and recovery of injured and sick persons and upon the possibility of giving to those suffering from partial infirmities, such as deafness, the chance of a happy and useful career. In time of mass unemployment those who are in receipt of compensation feel no urge to get well for idleness. On the other hand, in time of active demand for labour, as in war, the sick and the maimed are encouraged to recover, so that they may be useful.

Fourth, and most important, income security which is all that can be given by social insurance is so inadequate a provision for human happiness that to put it forward by itself as a sole or principal measure of reconstruction hardly seems worth doing. It should be accompanied by an announced determination to use the powers of the State to whatever extent may prove necessary to ensure for all, not indeed absolute continuity of work, but a reasonable chance of productive employment.

Fifth, though it should be within the power of the community to bear the cost of the whole Plan for Social Security, the cost is heavy and, if to the necessary cost waste is added, it may become insupportable. Unemployment, both through increasing expenditure on benefit and through reducing the income to bear those costs, is the worst form of waste.

441.   Assumption C does not imply complete abolition of unemployment. In industries subject to seasonal influences, irregularities of work are inevitable; in an economic system subject to change and progress, fluctuations in the fortunes of individual employers or of particular industries are inevitable; the possibility of controlling completely the major alternations of good trade and bad trade which are described under the term of the trade cycle has not been established; a country like Britain, which must have

exports to pay for its raw materials, cannot be immune from the results of changes of fortune or of economic policy in other countries. The Plan for Social Security provides benefit for a substantial volume of unemployment . . .

Assumption C requires not the abolition of all unemployment, but the abolition of mass unemployment and of unemployment prolonged year after year for the same individual. In the beginning of compulsory unemployment insurance in 1913 and 1914, it was found that less than 5 per cent. of all the unemployment experienced in the insured industries occurred after men had been unemployed for as long as 15 weeks. Even if it does not prove possible to get back to that level of employment, it should be possible to make unemployment of any individual for more than 26 weeks continuously a rare thing in normal times . . .

. . . 447. The rise in the general standard of living in Britain in the thirty or forty years that ended with the present war has two morals. First, growing general prosperity and rising wages diminished want, but did not reduce want to insignificance. The moral is that new measures to spread prosperity are needed. The Plan for Social Security is designed to meet this need; to establish a national minimum above which prosperity can grow, with want abolished. Second, the period covered by the comparisons between say 1900 and 1936 includes the first world war. The moral is the encouraging one, that it is wrong to assume that the present war must bring economic progress for Britain, or for the rest of the world, to an end.

449. The argument of this section can be summed up briefly. Abolition of want cannot be brought about merely by increasing production, without seeing to correct distribution of the product; but correct distribution does not mean what it has often been taken to mean in the past — distribution between the different agents in production, between land, capital, management and labour. Better distribution of purchasing power is required among wage-earners themselves, as between times of earning and not earning, and between times of heavy family responsibilities and of light or no family responsibilities. Both social insurance and children's allowances are primarily methods of re-distributing wealth. Such better distribution cannot fail to add to welfare and, properly designed, it can increase wealth, by maintaining physical vigour. It does not decrease wealth, unless it involves waste in administration or reduces incentives to production. Unemployment and disability are already being paid for unconsciously; it is no addition to the burden on the community to provide for them consciously. Unified social insurance will eliminate a good deal of waste inherent in present methods. Properly designed, controlled and financed, it need have no depressing effect on incentive . . .

(Beveridge, 1942, pp.153-4, 158-9, 163-4, 165, 166-7)

Our second extract is taken from William Robson's preface to a collection of Fabian essays on Social Security published in 1943. In this extract Robson draws attention to the similarity between the Fabian proposals and those set out in the Beveridge Report.

SAQ When reading this extract, you should note what conclusion Robson draws from this symmetry, about how social problems can be tackled.

Anyone who compares the Fabian scheme with the Beveridge Report will observe a large measure of agreement between them. The unification of administration in a new Ministry of Social Security; the assimilation of unemployment, sickness and disablement benefit in a new standard benefit; the payment of such benefit for the entire duration of unemployment or disability, subject to co-operation by the applicant in measures designed to set him on his feet again; the conversion of workmen's compensation from an affair of private rights, private finance and private conflicts into a publicly administered social insurance, and the assimilation (in 90 per cent. of the cases) of workmen's compensation with standard benefit for other disabilities; the provision of children's allowances as an essential aspect of family security; the introduction of maternity allowances for all gainfully occupied women and a maternity grant for all women; the payment of marriage allowances and burial allowances as a normal part of social insurance; recognition of the need to induce old persons to remain at work as long as they are willing and able to do so; an emphasis on the importance of the medical and industrial rehabilitation services, with special reference to training; the provision of a comprehensive medical service available to everyone without charge, and including hospital facilities and specialist treatment of all kinds; the reservation of widows' pensions for widows with dependent children and the treatment of other widows as persons requiring work or training; the replacement of public assistance by a residual service to meet abnormal cases on proof of need — on all these fundamental questions Sir William Beveridge and the authors of our scheme see eye to eye in principle, despite minor variations in detail . . .

   Taking the matter all in all, it is remarkable how large a measure of agreement exists between the Beveridge Report and the Fabian plan. That two bodies so differently constituted should reach identical conclusions in regard to so many of the fundamental issues is an encouraging sign of the times. It shows that, in this sphere at least, the rational method can point the way to a specific and inescapable programme of action. It demonstrates that if persons with qualified and trained minds will apply themselves in a disinterested manner to a great social problem of this kind, the proper principles will emerge so unmistakably that the right solution will cease to be a matter of mere opinion and become a question of scientific knowledge. It implies the beginning of a new outlook in the Social Sciences.

(Robson, 1943, pp. 2, 4-5)

The lesson which Robson identifies is a characteristically Fabian idea. Social problems can be solved through a 'rational method'. Qualified and trained minds, applied in a disinterested manner, can produce 'proper principles' — moving social problems from being a matter of opinion to the realm of scientific knowledge. This brief extract expresses the Fabian ideal of social reform.

   A further element of the Fabian tradition which can be discerned in the proposals of this period is the lack of 'enthusiasm for popular, democratic control of the services' (Mishra, 1981, p. 205). Our next extract is also taken from a Fabian essay on social security. This essay by John Clarke (no relation) deals with what the Fabians saw as central to state reform — the proper 'staffing' of the state.

SAQ What does Clarke identify as the desirable qualities for staff in a Ministry of Social Security?

A Ministry of Social Security will have to maintain close contact with numerous individual citizens, each of whom will judge the Ministry chiefly by his reception at the local office. It is of paramount importance to the Ministry that he should be welcomed and treated with consideration and interest. The reputation of the Ministry will depend largely on its local staff. These will have to be selected and appointed carefully, and it is essential to consider at the outset what sort of people they must be. But local staff, however suitable and expert, can only act within the framework of their Ministry's policy at any time. If the policy is ill-conceived, no local deftness will cover its deficiency . . .

On the other hand, in the long transmission belt carrying social policy from Whitehall to the private citizen, it is the interviewing officer who makes final delivery; if he is peremptory, hurried, irritable or stupid he will alienate citizens, and bungle the execution of policy however well thought out that policy may be. A Ministry of Social Security needs perpetual team-work between the planning and administrative Headquarters staff and the executives in all the local offices; each depends, for final success, upon the intelligent operations of the other. Each will benefit by close liaison — interchange between Headquarters and out-stations staff, Regional and local conferences, provincial officers of Headquarters type and calibre, an Intelligence staff which (among other duties) would explain policy to local staff, and, conversely, tell Headquarters planners how the public had reacted to new policy and what were current social trends.

The thesis of this chapter is that these various functions need persons specially equipped for their performance — that calculating widows' pension rates, relating size of benefits to population groups, estimating the effect of industrial planning on the volume of claims national and local, talking with deserted wives or pushing the malingerer back to work — that all these diverse jobs need special skills and special knowledge, and that both at its Headquarters and in its local offices the Ministry must appoint appropriate persons to exercise appropriate sorts of skill.

This cuts right across existing Whitehall theories and procedures; there seems to be a Civil Service tradition that if you set up tidy governmental machinery and recruit a body of intelligent administrators of high integrity, you can run anything — shipping, Cairo, coal-mines, pensions. The needs of economic planning in a technical age may prove this thesis wrong. Already the majority of higher appointments outside the Civil Service call both for technical specialisation and for background knowledge of economic, sociological, psychological or scientific processes.

. . . Expert administrative staff can prevent these sorts of confusion by weighing up future policy according to known social data and modern social science principles. It we are to plan our national social and economic policies we must have persons qualified to plan at all the planning points. The "born organiser," or the clever solicitor turned administrator, may be brilliant people, but if they lack economic knowledge where economic knowledge is essential, they are wrongly placed . . .

How are these sorts of experts to be got into the Ministry? In peace-time some of those who really understand the social sciences are congregated in the Universities; others are engaged on social surveys and research. Since the war many of them are temporary civil servants; they have been called in not only because administration has increased in scope, but because the urgency of war-time planning calls for the right people in the right places. If later we are to plan for national well-being the same criterion must carry over. We must have first-class persons where their skills are needed. We must be prepared to take economists, sociologists, psychologists and statisticians into the Ministry of Social Security at the higher salary ranges as temporary staff. We must be prepared to use suitable experts wherever they are to be found in the community. It is preposterous, for example, that an expert in social administration should be sent as government emissary to the West Indies, but that there should be no normal opportunity for him to occupy himself with government administration in this country. Such persons bring with them into government departments a range and depth of social experience which the professional civil servant lacks. In this respect they are likely at any time to be superior to the sociologist or economist who might, in a more enlightened future, be recruited straight into the administrative class from the University . . .

Recognition of the need for social science experts must be established straight away so that they may be incorporated into the new Ministry as soon as it is formed. "Good administrators" brought in from the higher ranks of other Ministries to start the new one will not suffice. It is essential that at least some of those who administer at the highest levels should understand the nature and the purpose of the social services.

(Clarke, 1943, pp. 373-5, 376-7)

Clarke begins by pointing to the need to have staff who will relate the new policies to the public, but by the end of the extract is asserting a powerful Fabian principle — the need for 'expertise'. Like Robson's 'qualified and disciplined minds' who can create rational solutions, for the Fabians, the solutions also need to be applied by qualified and disciplined minds.

Our final extract is taken from the autobiography of James Griffith, the Minister responsible for putting Beveridge's proposals into practice. The extract indicates how far the Beveridge Report (and its assumptions) dominated the political thinking of the Labour Party in this period.

Minister of National Insurance

1

'A REVOLUTIONARY moment in the world's history is a time for revolution — not for patching.'

This call for revolution came not from Moscow or Peking but from the one-time director of the London School of Economics, Sir William Beveridge, when he presented his plan for social security in 1942.

It was symbolic of the new revolution that the Minister of National Insurance, charged with the task of implementing the plan, and creating the Welfare State, should find himself installed at Carlton House Terrace, once the citadel of aristocratic power.

2

The Webbs, who lived in a world of Blue Books, once lamented that it took as long as thirty years before the recommendations of a royal commission were translated into legislation. The 1945 Labour Government boldly aimed to implement the Beveridge Plan in full within three years, and bring it into operation on the third anniversary of the great electoral victory — 5th July 1948.

This was a formidable task. It would necessitate five Acts of Parliament, scores of regulations and the creation of a nationwide organization.

Fortunately one of the five, the Family Allowances Act, was already on the statute book. The Americans have a custom of giving their legislation the names of sponsors in Congress, and it would have been appropriate to give the Family Allowances Act the name 'Eleanor Rathbone Act'. She had fought valiantly, against opposition from many quarters, for family endowment, and I had been one of her supporters in the many debates she initiated in the thirties.

Beveridge recommended allowances in cash at five shillings a week for every child in a family except the eldest, or only, child, and that this should be supplemented by services in kind to the value of three shillings per week.

I decided to bring family allowances into payment as soon as possible. My first job was to find the money, and I made the first of many visits to the Treasury. The Chancellor, Hugh Dalton, gave me the money, 'with a song in his heart', as he told our conference to the delight of our supporters and the fury of his critics.

It was not only in its cover that the [National Insurance] scheme broke new ground but also in the scope and variety of the benefits provided 'from the cradle to the grave'. It provided twice as many separate benefits as the old scheme and incorporated Beveridge's recommendation of a uniform standard for the principal benefits.

The 1946 [National Insurance] Act provided uniform benefits for sickness, unemployment and retirement, with dependants' benefits in each case. In addition it embodied Beveridge's recommendation that the amount of the major benefits should be such as would provide for basic needs, on a subsistence basis. I accept this basis.

The next question was how to ensure that the level would be maintained. This was, and has remained an unsolved problem. One of the practical difficulties is inherent in the insurance principle on which the scheme is based. I shared to the full Beveridge's view that benefits should be paid as of right on the basis of contributions and without any means test. My aim was to provide security with dignity. I considered the possibility of providing benefits on a sliding scale linked to the cost of living. This had practical difficulties in that it would require changes in contributions each time benefits were changed. I was reminded that when after 1918 war pensions had been tied to a cost of living scale it had worked well while the cost of living was rising and was abandoned the first time it fell. In the end, I provided in the Act that the minister should review the scale of benefits every five years with a view to adjusting them to changes in the cost of living and in the standard of life.

In the sphere of the social services the spirit of the administration is as important as the provisions of the legislation. I recognized that the ministry would be dealing with people in adversity, and that the qualities required of the staff were courtesy and dignity. . . .

5

While I was engaged in piloting the Insurance Bill through Parliament, Nye Bevan was triumphantly carrying through his bold and imaginative National Health Service Bill.

In the second session we joined forces in promoting the Bill to establish national assistance. The Bill aimed 'to terminate the existing poor law and to provide in lieu thereof for the assistance of persons in need by the National Assistance Board and by local authorities'. Responsibility for providing assistance in cash was transferred from the public assistance committees to a national board. The responsibility for welfare services for those who by 'age, infirmity or any other circumstances are in need' was to be entrusted to councils' welfare committees. We aimed to provide monetary payments and welfare services which would be different not only in their scope and provision, but also in the spirit in which they were administered.

. . . Beveridge called for a crusade to slay the five giant evils which afflicted our society — poverty, ignorance, disease, squalor and idleness. Within three years of our electoral victory, the Labour Government had provided the legislative framework and created the organization designed to rid our country of all five. To the Family Allowances Act we added four others — Industrial Injuries, National Insurance, National Health and National Assistance. During those same years Ellen Wilkinson and George Tomlinson, at the Ministry of Education, began to implement the 1944 Education Act. The school-leaving age was raised to fifteen, and it was planned eventually to raise it to sixteen.

Together these six Acts of Parliament provide the foundation of Britain's Welfare State. To those of us who were privileged to take part in this work, the Welfare State was not a luxury dependent on what was left over in the national Treasury but the first call upon our resources. To those others who, at that time and now, persist in deriding the security of the Welfare State, I would say as I did to the House of Commons in 1946:

> For a generation I have lived with the consequences of insecurity. To those who profess to fear that security will weaken the moral fibre and destroy self respect, let me say this. It is insecurity that destroys. It is fear of tomorrow that paralyses the will. It is the frustration of human hopes that corrodes the soul. Security will release our people from the haunting fears of yesterday, and their gifts to the service of the nation.

In his report Beveridge warned us that 'freedom from want cannot be forced on a democracy, it must be won by them'.

The scene at the Empress Ballroom, Blackpool, as Labour makes its plans for power, 9th June 1945

In the nineteen-forties we fought and won a battle for the cause of social security. We rejoice that the present generation knows not the poverty and distress of the thirties.

(Griffiths, 1969, pp. 79, 80-1, 84-7, 88-9)

How then, can we sum up the Fabian conception of welfare in this period? The most significant single issue is that Fabianism was almost completely tied to the Beveridge Report, finding itself in total agreement with Beveridge's approach and proposals. This unity is not particularly surprising. Although Beveridge stood as a Liberal in the 1945 elections, he had, since the turn of the century been associated with leading Fabians, particularly the Webbs, and his approach to 'social problems' had been strongly influenced by this association.

SAQ What welfare did the Fabians believe should be provided?

As we have noted above, the Fabians accepted Beveridge's conception of a 'national minimum' dealing with families, health and unemployment. They also supported Beveridge's commitment to a rationally managed economy (through the application of Keynesianism) to ensure full employment.

SAQ What did they identify as causing the need for welfare provision?

Beveridge's distinction again forms the basis for the Fabians. Mass unemployment is to be avoided by government economic policy. This was identified as the major cause of distress in the nineteen-thirties. By contrast, the welfare state was designed to cope with *temporary* interruptions of employment (ill health and individual unemployment). It was also intended to support the family in its task of bringing up children, by providing financial and material support to the mother whose primary function was caring for children.

SAQ How was welfare provision to be provided?

The detail of reports and arguments makes it clear that the era of the expert had arrived. Even outside of official reports, such as Beveridge's, the tone is quite clear. Carefully argued, couched in terms of legal enactments and the language of officialdom. Somehow the apparently dull language of Beveridge was translated into the excitement of political demands and somehow the excitement of these demands was translated back into the language of official reports and the search for good administrators. Welfare was to be the sphere of professionals apparently working according to agreed principles, and there was little thought about means of democratic control or informed debate. Once the broad principles had been agreed that could safely be left to the experts.

---

3 SOCIALISM

As we have seen, the socialists were generally swept up in the enthusiasm for Beveridge. But two *caveats* need to be placed against this statement. First, there remained a group, no matter how small, who remained opposed to the palliatives of reform and who continued to insist on the need for social revolution. (Reports from Mass Observation, quoted in Addison, 1977, p. 245, indicate that these attitudes were not as restricted as written evidence suggests). Second, some socialists saw Beveridge as a means to push for a new society. For them, Beveridge was a stepping stone rather than an end in itself. It showed the extent to which Britain's rulers were being forced to go in the context of social upheaval. They must be forced to carry out the policy, and then to go beyond it.

The first extract from the Socialist Party of Great Britain indicates the view of the first group of socialists described above. For them, the Labour Party in government was simply carrying out the dirty work for the capitalists, making a few concessions, but above all preparing the way for normal service and Conservative rule to be resumed as soon as possible. They argued that not only were palliatives not enough and weakened the political resistance of workers but also that some of the 'reforms' were positively harmful. This extract focuses on family allowances. Eleanor Rathbone's arguments, some of which you met in Unit 2, are explicitly criticized. You should contrast the SPGB's criticisms of family allowances with the ways in which feminists criticize the Beveridge proposals in Section 3.

SAQ What are the main criticisms levelled at family allowances in this extract?

The claim that schemes for social reform can eradicate some or all of the worst evils of Capitalism has often been made in the past and just as often proved to be false. The present war has provided a fertile breeding ground for plans for abolishing the slums, establishing permanent peace on earth, removing the degradation accompanying old age and unemployment, improving the health of the workers and so on. The production of these plans should be expected at a time when many workers are extremely sceptical as to the outcome of the war in connection with their own conditions of life and wondering, in fact, if after this war things are going to be measurably better than they were after that of 1914-18 . . .

In support of Family Allowances advocates claim that their introduction will abolish a major part of poverty, on the ground that the principal cause of poverty is the possession of young families.

We state immediately that no scheme for social reform can remove the poverty endured by the working-class under Capitalism. The poverty of the working-class is as constant a condition of Capitalism as the never ending flow of pettifogging schemes for the alleviation of poverty which the workers are asked to support . . .

It does not necessarily follow that reforms can never be of any benefit to the workers, although it is true to say that reforms cannot abolish the major evils of Capitalism, nor will they generally be introduced to deal with some of the minor evils except when their introduction is necessary to ensure the continued smooth running of the capitalist system. There are, however, some proposals for social reform which may be harmful in themselves, and perhaps the most obnoxious of all are those which on the surface appear philanthropic, but which in effect work towards a lowering of the already low standard of living of the working-class. We may place in this category the schemes that have been put forward from time to time for Family Allowances.

The Family Allowance advocates claim (to quote one of the best known, Sir William Beveridge, a Vice-President of the Family Endowment Society), letter to *Times* of January 12th, 1960:—

". . . the greatest single cause of poverty in this country is young children."

They further state that as industry in this country is unable to afford a general increase in wages, this poverty can only be abolished by a scheme whereby parents with dependent children would receive allowances over and above their wages. We will deal later with the assertion that industry in this country is unable to afford a general increase in wages, but we challenge immediately the statement that "the greatest single cause of poverty in this country is young children."

Professor Colin Clark (People's Year Book, 1936) stated that 850,000 persons with over £500 a year shared between them a total almost as great as that which was shared between 12,000,000 people with incomes below £122 a year.

G. W. Daniels and H. Campion (The Distribution of National Capital, Manchester University Press, 1936) showed that 1 per cent. of the persons aged 25 or over in England and Wales owned 60 per cent. of the total national capital of about £14,000,000,000, or on a slightly broader basis 5 per cent. owned 80 per cent. of the total national capital.

Here is disclosed the real poverty of the working population, besides which the difference in the conditions of those workers with families to support and those without appears trivial and insignificant. The social chasm between rich and poor is thrown into even sharper relief when it is recognised that the vast mass of the impoverished workers perform all of the useful work of society, whilst the privileged minority can be, and generally are, idle and unproductive.

If the advocates of Family Allowances are sincere in their expressed desire to abolish poverty we would draw their attention to this, the "greatest single," and in fact the only, cause of poverty in the modern world against which they might direct their attacks.

It is questionable, however, whether all of those who have most assiduously supported Family Allowances have been actuated entirely by a desire to improve the lot of sections of the workers. Some years ago Miss Eleanor Rathbone, M.P., who is chairman of the Family Endowment Society, explained to some of the business men of the insurance world at the Annual Conference of the Faculty of Insurance that in the case of a contributory scheme for Family Allowances the burden would fall on the "young men and the young women who nearly all are going to get married pretty soon and have dependent children, and who would be expected to be willing to make some sacrifice at the expense of their cigarettes, cinemas, and betting on football to provide for the period when the children are coming along." (Journal of the Faculty of Insurance, July 1927.) . . .

The problem that Miss Rathbone touched upon in her address to the insurance fraternity was in fact not so much that workers with family responsibilities do not receive enough, but, from the Capitalist point of view the much more serious one that workers without families are receiving too much!

It might at first sight appear paradoxical to assert that a saving in the total national wage bill can be effected by additional payments being made to certain sections of the workers, but in the long run such a saving will result from the introduction of Family Allowances. As soon as the cost (or perhaps more truly the "alleged" cost) of rearing some or all of the workers' children is considered by the employers to have been provided for outside of wages, the tendency will assert itself for wages to sink to a new level based on the cost of maintaining a worker and his wife, or a worker, his wife and one child as the case may be.

The most obvious way in which this reduction may come about is by introducing Family Allowances at a time when prices have risen instead of granting a general increase in wages to meet the increased cost of living. Sir W. Beveridge admitted this possibility when replying to a question put to him at a meeting of civil servants at Central Hall, Westminister, January 28th, 1943. He said:—

> "I do not see why the provision of Family Allowances should decrease salaries and wages. The possibility that they might lead to wages not going up so quickly is no reason for not providing adequately for children first."

(Whitley Bulletin, March, 1943.)

The recent decision of the Trades Union Congress to support Family Allowances will render it easier for the employers to give an imaginary sop to a small fraction of the workers, whilst, in fact, the large majority have suffered a setback. . . .

But the real issue is not that certain unscrupulous employers may seek to save out of wages amounts paid in Family Allowances, but that once it is established that the children (or some of the children) of the workers have been "provided for" by other means, the tendency will be for wage levels to sink to new standards which will not include the cost of maintaining such children. . . .

Miss Rathbone thus sees in Family Allowances a means whereby a revolution can be averted and it is beside the point that she attributed to the Labour Party intentions which they themselves would probably be the first to deny. This theme is also touched upon in her book, "The Case for Family Allowances" (1940, Penguin), where she claims that the preservation of family life by means of Family Allowances may quite well be "a bulwark against certain explosive and disrupting forces. A man with a wife and family may talk revolution, but he is much less likely to act it than one who has given Society no such hostages." P. 14.)

We are quite certain that neither Family Allowances nor any other sop offered to the workers can in the long run prevent the growth of ideas which will lead to the disruption of the capitalist system, but we take note that here again, mingled with Miss Rathbone's professed desire to improve the lot of certain sections of the working-class, there appears a motive of quite a different order.

(SPGB, undated, pp. 2, 5-7, 8-9, 11-15)

There seem to be three main points here. First, it is erroneous to think about eliminating poverty while the fundamental inequality of wealth remains untouched. Second, capitalists would use the introduction of family allowances to reduce the wages of the working class. Finally, reforms like these are a palliative to shore up an unequal society, and prevent social revolution.

Our second extract, from *Tribune,* reflects a rather different socialist response. Here, the Beveridge Report is treated as confirming socialist arguments, and thus becomes a valuable weapon in the socialist armoury.

Beveridge Manifesto

In a general sense the decision to allow a report on social conditions to appear at this time was the work of a guilty national conscience. No return to the conditions of the past were thought possible. The Left were demanding the pledge of a new world. The Right (in the days of military inactivity) realised the perils of withstanding concession. No doubt they believed that a goodly array of burnished platitudes would stay the avalanche of public opinion until they were stronger for the fight and until their conscience had relapsed into its old accustomed inertia. Nothing else can explain the political lunacy (from their own point of view) of Mr Churchill and his friends which has tolerated the publication of Sir William's findings. For the mouse has been in labour and has brought forth a mountain.

Sir William Beveridge is a social evangelist of the old Liberal school. He is an honoured member of the Reform Club, and the horizon of his political aspirations is, therefore, not boundless. He specifically disavows many of the tenets of revolutionary Socialism. But he has a good heart and a clear, well-stocked head, and he has discharged his task with Liberal fervour and even a trace of Liberal innocence.

What kind of world would the honest Liberal like to establish? He would like to make a truce between private enterprise and State ownership. He would like the two to work in harness together, but, above all, he would like, by resolute action, to appease the most obvious pains and to succour the most grievous casualties which capitalism produces. From this dangerous angle Sir William has approached his task. He would like to establish a tolerable minimum standard of security for every citizen, for the injured worker, for the widow, for the aged, for the unemployed, for the sick and for the growing child.

This is a commendable ambition, and the desire to achieve it is certainly not confined to those who have dabbled or delved into Socialism. But the merit and novelty of Sir William is that he has set down with the authority of a statistician and on Government note-paper the conditions which must be satisfied if this modest ambition is to be achieved. Here it is in black and white — a plain description of man's necessities, how much (or how little) he must have in his pocket if fear and want and hunger are to be lifted from his cares and if the grandiloquent phrases of the Atlantic Charter are to be translated into fact. In short, Sir William has described the conditions in which the tears might be taken out of capitalism. We should not be surprised, therefore, if all unconsciously by so doing he threatens capitalism itself.

Sir William states plainly that human claims must come first. The miner choked by silicosis, the worker who loses a finger in his machine, the old man and his wife who have done their lifetime of service, the widow who has lost her husband, the husband whose job has become momentarily redundant, the child whose parents cannot give him the best, none of these and none of the others who have suffered the disabilities of our society in the past must suffer in the future. It is an outrage that men should be the victims of these harrowing fears. To keep their bodies healthy, to ease their minds, to release their souls — these are the first claims on the State. The claim of property must come second . . .

It will still be a battle, but we must thank Sir William for a weapon. And if it be asked how it happens that a reformer so sedate has been able to fashion a weapon so sharp, and how a Government so timid should have presented materials for its fashioning, we must answer in the famous words of Karl Marx, 'that war is the locomotive of history' . . .

(Hill, 1977)

SAQ Was there any difference between the 'Tribune' response to Beveridge and that of the Fabians?

We think the answer here has to be 'yes, but . . .' Yes it was different because 'Tribune' was concerned to use it and push for it as a propaganda weapon in the broader fight for socialism. In fact the left doubted whether Beveridge or anything like it could really be carried through under capitalism. But, 'Tribune' made no basic criticisms of the report or the assumptions which underly it, whether on family allowances or anything else. They, too, seemed to accept that a growth of the state and state officials must in itself imply some benevolent process which should, therefore, be supported.

Socialists, then, were once again divided by the issue of reform. For some, Beveridge represented a potential stepping stone on the road to a socialist society, while for others, it meant a reform which would temporarily block the development of a social revolution.

4 FEMINISM

4.1 '1945' AND FEMINISM

Amongst the general acclaim which greeted the Beveridge Report, there were voices of discontent and criticism from the ranks of the feminists in 1945. They did not argue simply that certain provisions were not adequate, nor that in certain respects the Report did not go far enough. They criticized one of the basic assumptions of the Report, namely that married women should be treated as a special category, obliged to be dependent on their husbands for economic survival.

It must be realised that Beveridge was not the first to treat married women as dependent housewives, Lloyd George's insurance scheme had done so in 1911, and had been criticized by feminists then. But the significance of the Beveridge Report was that it constructed an interdependent network of welfare benefits and schemes including sickness benefits, unemployment benefits, pensions, family allowances and maternity benefits which all rested on the crucial distinction between married women and other adults. This special consideration to married women was articulated as a benevolent recognition of the housewife's vital (but unpaid) contributions to the nation's health and welfare. Discriminatory treatment was presented as a reward.

What angered the feminists in 1945 was the way in which Beveridge (a) praised the housewife but did nothing practical to help her and (b) the way he denied women any financial independence once they were married. What is interesting is that they did not in general dispute Beveridge's ideal of marriage as a team, nor did they argue with the assumption that childcare and housework should be the wife's responsibility on a practical and day-to-day level.

The following quotes from the Report give a flavour of Beveridge's stance on marriage. Note the moral tone that is assumed and the ideological assumption that women are the carriers of culture and standards.

In any measure of social policy in which regard is had to facts, the great majority of married women must be regarded as occupied on work which is vital though unpaid, without which their husbands could not do their paid work and without which the nation could not continue. In accord with facts the Plan for Social Security treats married women as a special insurance class of occupied persons and treats man and wife as a team.

(Beveridge, 1942, p. 49)

During marriage most women will not be gainfully employed. The small minority of women who undertake paid employment or other gainful occupations after marriage require special treatment differing from that of a single woman. Since such paid work will in many cases be intermittent, it should be open to any married woman to undertake it as an exempt person, paying no contributions of her own and acquiring no claim to benefit in unemployment or sickness. If she prefers to contribute and to requalify for unemployment and disability benefit she may do so but will receive benefits at a reduced rate.

(Op cit, p. 50)

That attitude of the housewife to gainful employment outside the home is not and *should not* be the same as that of the single women. She has other duties ... Taken as a whole the Plan for Social Security puts a premium on marriage in place of penalising it ... In the next thirty years housewives as *Mothers* had vital work to do in ensuring the adequate continuance of the British Race and of British *Ideals* in the world.

(Op cit, p. 52, emphasis added)

This is not to argue that the Report and the 1946 National Insurance Act did not improve social conditions for both men and women. In fact the Women's TUC supported Beveridge precisely because it offered working class women better security and better health and maternity provisions than they had experienced before. The Report was 'better than nothing' for the majority of women and no doubt attempts to criticize it were seen as anti-progressive and anti-working class. However, some feminists did object to it, even though their voices were hardly heard over the approving choruses from the TUC and other bodies. Before outlining the feminist position on Beveridge however, it is perhaps necessary to consider briefly the nature of feminism in the 1940s and 1950s.

Studies of this period (Wilson, 1980; Birmingham Feminist History Group (1979)) suggest that feminism then was radically different from pre-World War I and contemporary feminisms. In fact it is probably inaccurate to talk of a feminist *movement* in the 1940s and 1950s. Certainly some of the original suffrage groups remained intact, for example, the Six Point Group (SPG), the Women's Freedom League (WFL) and the Women's Co-operative Guild. All of these organizations had become less radical, although this is not to imply that they could not muster formidable opposition to Beveridge and other social insurance schemes. In addition to these long established groups there were newer organizations who were much less radical than their predecessors. The Married Women's Association (MWA), founded in 1938 by Juanita Frances, for example aimed to transform marriage into an equal partnership, rather than to challenge the concept and basis of marriage. The Council of Married Women founded in 1952, proposed to go further and support the 'stabilisation and dignity of marriage as an institution'. Women for Westminster, as its name implies, was solely concerned with increasing the political and democratic participation of women at all levels of Government. It was founded in 1942 by Mrs Rebecca Sieff, Dr Edith Summerskill and Mrs Corbett Ashby with the specific desire to include women in the reconstruction of Britain after the war.

Undoubtedly feminism, even of this fairly mild variety, was on the decline after the war. After two wars in fairly quick succession with only a period of deep economic recession in between, it is perhaps not surprising that feminism found it difficult to thrive. The period of reconstruction after the war was based on an ideal of 'working together' to improve the quality of life. It was consequently quite difficult for feminists to oppose this ideology and even where they were critical they did not challenge the values of family life and marriage.

While the early feminists concentrated on graphic descriptions of the oppression of mainly poor women in marriage and later feminists identified the family as the primary site of women's oppression, feminists in the '40s tended to celebrate the role of wife and mother. They were not, however, insensitive to new measures or legislation which tried to exploit the duties of motherhood and which failed to give wives and mothers the protection they needed in the event of family or marriage break-down or the hardship of poverty.

As the Beveridge Plan gathered momentum and trade union and Labour Party support, so opposition to it from women's organizations grew proportionately until in 1944 twelve of the major groups united to present a deputation to the government. In the same year, Edith Summerskill, a Labour MP as well as a feminist, presented a petition containing 77,000 signatures demanding justice for wives under the social insurance scheme. Their anger against the scheme is best articulated in a pamphlet by two feminists, Elizabeth Abbott and Katherine Bompas (1943), both of the WFL.

SAQ When reading this extract you should specifically look out for:

1 how the authors argue that financial independence will improve marriage (rather than undermine it);

2 how they criticize the Report for encouraging women to give up their rights, for example through the obviously attractive facility of paying lower National Insurance rates; and

3 how they emphasize the need for responsibility for married women which is denied them in the Report. In this respect they adopt a particularly moral tone which gives an insight into their views on the value of women's work.

You will see that at the beginning and the end of the pamphlet Abbott and Bompass make it plain that on the whole the Report is a 'good thing' so they are not criticizing it from an anti-welfare or conservative position. They also make several recommendations for improving the plan. While reading these proposals try to work out how many had been implemented by 1980, this should give an indication of the difficulty feminists have faced in trying to win acceptance for their ideas.

The Women Citizen and Social Security

There has been, and rightly, a marked unanimity in welcoming the Beveridge Report as to many of its details and in general as an effort to establish security for those who suffer from unemployment or disability in the course of their working lives, to help in some measure all who are in need, and to provide independence in old age.

It must be made plain from the outset, therefore, that criticism of the Beveridge Report as a whole is not the aim of this Memorandum, which is confined to questioning the justice, realism and social effects of the insurance and social service proposals made for women, and in particular for married women, whether they be workers or housewives.

It is where the Plan falls short of being really national in character, where it shuts out or exempts from all direct participation over nine million adult women, where it imposes special financial burdens on men alone, instead of spreading them equitably over all, that it fails and is open to criticism.

The error — an error which lies in the moral rather than the economic sphere [sic] — lies in denying to the married woman, rich or poor, housewife or paid worker, an independent personal status. From this error springs a crop of injustices, complications and difficulties, personal, marital and administrative, involving in the long run men both married and unmarried, and the unmarried as well as the married women.

If it be suggested that in the past the housewives of the nation have not been insured, and that as long as any of the present framework of the insurance system remains it would be difficult to insure them directly, two comments must be made. First, the general aim of the new security plan is to get away from what has been bad and inefficient in the past. Instead of getting away from the bad past in this respect, the Plan has shaken hands with it and made a poor compromise.[1] And secondly, a new Social Security Plan which makes recommendations — whether they are accepted or not is beside the point — so revolutionary as to involve the liquidation of a vast sphere of business in the Industrial Assurance Companies and the medical profession as at present organised, could well have made proposals for the insurance of women more in harmony with their changed and changing status in the social order.

It must be emphasised, then, that it is not upon the denial of equal economic status to women that the Plan comes to grief. Indeed the unmarried woman worker has equal economic status but is divorced from equal responsibility. It is with the denial of any personal status to a woman because she is married, the denial of her independent personality within marriage, that everything goes wrong and becomes unjust and ungenerous, sometimes comic, always unrealistic and inevitably antagonistic to the best interests of marriage and social life. In place of the famous phrase of Blackstone: "I and my wife are one, and I am he," the author of the Report has substituted his special version: "Every woman on marriage becomes a new person." Nearly two hundred years my lie between the two phrases. The thought behind them is the same: that a married woman is not a person at all. To-day, as so many years ago, injustice and complication are the inevitable result. That this may be quite other than the aim of the Plan is apparent, since its author refers to the married woman as "an equal partner," as "occupied on work which is vital," etc. etc. The tribute of the word is a sad common place to women. What is here of concern is not what the Report may say in praise of women, but what it proposes shall be done and the social tendencies which will be thereby encouraged. Far from putting a premium on marriage, as it purports to do, the Plan penalises both the married woman and marriage itself.

Summary of Points to be Criticised

A. Unequal retirement age.

B. (1) Loss of insurance rights on marriage.
   (2) Loss of contributions paid by women from 16 until marriage.
   (3) Marriage Grant.

C. Housewives' insurance: The Housewife's Policy.

D. (1) Option of the gainfully occupied married women to exempt herself from insurance.
   (2) Lower benefits for the gainfully occupied and fully insured married woman.

E. Uncertain position of unpaid domestic workers who are not the wives of insured men.

F. The view that Maternity Grant and Benefit are a woman's benefit.

G. (1) Exception of the married woman (housewife or exempt worker) from retirement age of 60.
   (2) Loss of individual pension paid for by contributions from the married woman insured worker on her husband's retirement.

H. The position of the unmarried woman earner: an equal benefit for a lower contribution. Economic equality without equal responsibility.

I. The unequal moral standard as applied to the married woman, the unmarried mother and the woman living as a wife . . .

B. (1) **LOSS OF INSURANCE RIGHTS BY EVERY WOMAN ON MARRIAGE.**
   (2) **LOSS OF ALL CONTRIBUTIONS MADE BY A WOMAN PRIOR TO MARRIAGE**
   (3) **PROPOSED MARRIAGE GRANT.**

(1 & 2) Loss of Insurance Rights on Marriage and of all contributions made prior to marriage.

These proposals must be unconditionally rejected. The loss of insurance rights and of pre-marriage contributions is not a new proposal. It was put forward and rejected before the introduction of the Anomalies Act. The Report proposes to abolish the Anomalies Regulations for married women — regulations which were both foolish and unjust — and to substitute a still greater injustice. Onerous and unfair as these Regulations were, the married woman worker at any rate retained her position as an insured person, with the right to benefit *under certain conditions.* The new proposal is that every woman on marriage shall lose her accumulated payments (spreading in many cases over ten years or more) and cease to be an insured person. Should she remain in work or take fresh work, she has to requalify for insurance, and is then put in a position as regards benefit inferior to any other adult worker (16/- instead of 24/-).

It is important that people should not make fraudulent insurance claims. It is far more important that the State should not adopt fraudulent insurance schemes. The intelligent citizen, man or woman, may well view with surprise the statement in the Report that "on marriage every woman will become a new person," when in fact the Plan ensures that a woman on marrying ceases to be a person at all.

(3) The Marriage Grant. This is offered up to £10 as a solace for the loss of insurance rights and accumulated payments on marriage. It is not an integral part of the scheme and should be rejected both in its intention and in the form in which it is offered. *The consequences of selling a birthright for a mess of pottage are well known, and women would do well to remember that rights once lost are hard to recover.*

If it is desired to encourage marriage, a Joint Marriage Grant to the contracting parties is the proper form for such endowment to take.

The Real Position of the Housewife.

The real position of the housewife under the Plan can best be realised by comparing the treatment of the two partners in "the team" at the moment when one or other falls sick.

When the man is ill he gets 24/- for himself and 16/- for his wife, plus the full benefits of the New National Health Service, and if he is not in hospital, a free nurse in the person of his wife.

When the woman is ill, she also gets the advantages of the National Health Service, since that is to be available to every individual citizen. She gets no penny of cash and if ill in her own home, is supposed to be able to get "neighbourly and family help" (par. 244). This is the moment when — as those who know the lives of working people realise — the woman would find extra money invaluable. It might be the one means of securing that friendly or family help which is needed.

The new scheme for housewives should be rejected and with it the housewives' policy which is no more than a scrap of paper. Is it not time for the recognition of some plain facts? Though the married woman is not gainfully occupied in the sense that she earns money by salary or by profits from the sale of goods, she is a gainfully occupied person. Her livelihood is the occupation of housekeeping, as a partner in marriage, and in that partnership she has a definite financial share as a worker. In addition to that work which has this definite financial value, she is the mother of the sons and daughters of the nation.

The Report truly says that without the work of such women men could not do their paid work nor the nation continue; and calls upon them to ensure not only the continuance of the British race but the continuance of British ideals in the world. Their value is recognised in words. But there is no practical recognition of the needs of this central figure in our social economy. No independent status is given to her as citizen and worker, no real amelioration of the difficulties of her life . . .

D. THE GAINFULLY OCCUPIED MARRIED WOMAN

i.   Her option to exempt herself from insurance.
ii. Lower cash benefits for the married woman worker paying full contributions.

Par. 343. The proposal that a married woman who takes gainful employment should be able to exempt herself from contributions (though her employer continues to contribute) must be rejected unconditionary. It is one of the most reactionary proposals in the Report. It cuts at the root of the principle on which national insurance has been and is based: the compulsory insurance at least of all citizen workers (Class I in this Report).

This retrograde proposals creates (and perhaps is intended to create) the married women worker as a class of pin-money worker, whose work is of so little value to either the community or herself, that she need feel no responsibility either for herself as an individual or as a member of society towards a scheme which purports to bring about national security for all citizens.

The report argues generally that the married woman does not need the same benefits, and in particular that she is not responsible for the payment of rent. This is to confuse the principles of insurance with those of Assistance. Insurance benefits are normally based on the rates of contribution, and equal contributions must entail equal benefits. Once a general plan and general rates are adopted these being based on average needs, the question of individual need is wholly out of place. This the Report recognises in every other instance. The argument as to rent is not only unrealistic, it is rejected in the Report (par. 210) as presenting very great administrative difficulties when other members of the family, or lodgers, are concerned. It is used as an excuse for depriving the married woman of the benefits for which she has paid . . .

F. MATERNITY GRANT AND BENEFIT

The Report deems these to be women's benefits. It fails to recognise that parenthood is a joint affair and that the well-being of mother and child are the concern, not of the woman alone, but of the husband and father and also of society as a whole. These are Family Benefits. They should be so regarded and should be paid out of the contributions of the whole community plus the appropriate contribution from the Exchequer. No social plan should fail to place emphasis on joint parental responsibility. Such emphasis is properly secured not by words of admonition to women on their duties, but by a recognition of the equal obligation of both parents.

This Maternity Benefit of 36/- a week for 13 weeks for the gainfully occupied woman, conditional on her giving up her paid work, is a new proposal, and one doubtless of excellent intention. It might indeed have a certain value, if unconditional, for women earning a very low wage at intermittent or unhealthy work. But for the better paid woman in a light or healthy job earning anything from £3 a week upwards, 36/- a week plus the loss of her job is not a helpful or realistic proposal. It may be argued that it is "better than nothing" but, as always, "the better is the enemy of the good." When as at present there is a widespread demand for "a keener and more generous public recognition of motherhood as an honourable duty and profession," (The Times, 23.9.43. Letter; A.V. Hill) proposals touching parenthood which are only "better than nothing" are not good enough, and no proposal should begin by limiting the personal rights of one of the parents — the mother . . .

CONCLUSION

Reference has already been made to the good and progressive features of the Report as a whole, and the fact that many women will be helped in various ways, some directly, as by the equal benefits for single women; others indirectly by the extension of the health service to the woman in the home;

others by the realistic and just reform of widowhood aid and the plan for bringing younger widows back into employment.

Nevertheless, the scheme as a whole is marred by the general plan for insuring women, particularly the married woman.

The critic is too often denounced for not being creative, and there is a tendency to ignore the fact that demolitions and constructions are rarely carried out by the same hands. This Memorandum has dealt with what is considered to be a basic failure in the Plan; the failure to treat women as full and independent fellow citizens with men. It offers only general recommendations which are set forth below. The exact method by which these ends are to be attained cannot be indicated in detail. The necessary readjustments throughout the scheme would have to be framed by experts, including a readjustment of the actuarial basis of the scheme.

Recommendations

1 An equal retirement age.

2 Safeguarding of pension and other rights of unpaid domestic workers by compulsory insurance on their behalf.

3 Direct insurance of the married woman — the housewife — with benefits adjusted to her needs, including cash benefit when she is disabled by sickness or accident and retirement pension in her own right.

4 Maintenance of insurance rights upon marriage, subject to general tests of genuine desire for the availability for work.

5 No exemption from insurance of the married woman worker, save the general exemption for any person who earns less than £75 a year.

6 Full normal benefit for the married woman worker when unemployed or disabled.

7 Full pension in her own right for the insured married woman.

8 Payment by single women of an equal contribution for an equal benefit.

9 Removal from the Plan of all moral tests.

10 Widowhood benefit should be recognised as and called Temporary Loss of Livelihood Benefit.

11 Maternity Grant and Benefit and Guardian Benefit should be acknowledged for what they are: not individual benefits, but Family Benefits, designed to safeguard the bearing, rearing, sustenance, health, home life and general well-being of children.

Practically all the disabilities and anomalies criticised could have been obviated had there been a different approach to the whole subject. *At present the Plan is mainly a man's plan for man:* it remains selective instead of being truly national. A great part of what is offered to women is in the spirit of that *mistaken benevolence* from which perhaps more than anything else women need to be emancipated before they can take their place as partners in marriage and in work. Henry James' father once wrote:

> "I have so long been accustomed to see the most arrant deviltry transact itself in the name of benevolence that the moment I hear a profession of good will from almost any quarter I instinctively look about for a constable or place my hand within reach of the bell-rope. . . I do hope that the reign of benevolence is over; until that occurs I am sure the reign of God is impossible."

Therein lies a deep truth, upon which everyone of us in these days would do well to ponder. One thing is certain. To continue to give women what seems to others to be good for them; to give them indeed anything with an ulterior motive be it the preservation of marriage and the family, or a rise in the birth rate — is doomed to failure. To respect women as individuals, to give them what is their right as citizens and workers, may, on the other hand, have great and beneficial effect far beyond any immediate object. For both security and progress are rooted in justice.

(Abbott and Bompas, 1943, emphasis added)

The criticisms here focus particularly on the Report's proposals for married women. They contrast the Report's rhetoric about the value and importance of the wife and mother with the proposals which fail to treat her as an independent person. This stress on the need for treating the married woman as an independent person is not from a position which is against marriage. On the contrary, the authors argue that, for the partnership of marriage to work well, married women must be treated as independent so that they can contribute properly to the partnership.

(You may wish to note that women have still to achieve recommendations 1, 2, 3, 4 and 6. Point 9 was dropped before the plan became legislation and it referred to insuring married women against marital breakdown as long as they were the innocent party. It also concerned unmarried mothers who had no husbands through whom they could claim maternity benefits. It is unlikely that feminists today would support points 10 and 11 in the form they are advocated here but regardless of this they have not been achieved. Only points 7 and 8 have been fully achieved.)

Many of the criticisms that feminists levelled against the Beveridge plan were not published but simply argued in public meetings or at committee meetings. Probably all the feminist groups at the time discussed the plan but we have selected one extract from the weekly bulletin of the Women's Freedom League. Their comments are necessarily brief but it is possible to recognise that the WFL's position was slightly more radical than that adopted by Abbott and Bompas (even though they were members of the WFL).

SAQ Consider their eight points and compare them with the points put forward by Abbott and Bompas. In particular consider the WFL's first point which is a goal that contemporary feminists are still urging. In this demand the WFL not only require financial independence to be granted by the state but also reject the ideology of marriage as a team effort.

The Beveridge Report

The Women's Freedom League looks forward to the plan for Social Security to be evolved by Parliament on the basis of the Beveridge Report on condition, however, that it provides a fair field and no favour for women. The broad fundamental principles are generally accepted:

Flat rate of subsistence benefit
Flat rate of contribution
Unification of administrative responsibility
Adequacy of benefit
Comprehensiveness
Classification

But the W.F.L. wishes to offer very definite suggestions without which the cause of women will not receive justice. Take the question of classification. It is true that the community is divided into employees, others gainfully occupied, others of working age, below working age, retired above working age, but we would substitute for "housewives", "others non-gainfully occupied".

We actually demand:

1 *That men and women should in marriage not be treated as a "team" but as individuals each paying equal contributions and receiving equal benefits; and that in every case men and women should pay the same and receive the same benefits.*
2 That women in insurance before marriage should not terminate that insurance on marriage but should continue as direct contributors as above; and that therefore there should be no marriage grant.

3   That unmarried women doing unpaid domestic work should be brought into the compulsory scheme, paying equal contributions and receiving equal benefits.

4   That gainfully employed married women who pay equal contributions should receive equal benefits. (Maternity grant and benefit should form part of the general health scheme).

5   That the minimum age for retirement benefits or pension should be 60 for both men and women, a married woman being a direct contributor would therefore, if she wishes, get her pension, at that age regardless of the age of her husband.

6   The 13 weeks' benefit at a higher rate on widowhood is approved and it is suggested that some comparable grant be made to a widower.

7   The Guardianship allowance for widows with dependant children is approved. This should also apply to unmarried mothers where it would benefit the child. The training benefit for widows is approved.

8   In regard to compulsion to take other work after a period on unemployment benefit where no openings exist in usual employment, together with compulsory training, the alternative work should be reasonably comparable with normal employment and standard of living, and there should be full safeguards through appeal to a tribunal.

These recommendations were formulated at a meeting of members and approved by the Executive Committee of the N.F.L. on January 12th 1943. They have been sent to the Government and to the women Members of Parliament.

Will all readers study them and try to get their own M.P.s to support the demands made when the Beveridge Report comes up for debate in Parliament?

(Women's Freedom League, 1943a, emphasis added)

The argument that married men and women should be treated as 'individuals' in insurance and benefit plans may seem only to be a logical extension of the demand for 'women's independence'. But it is important to note that this demand is made explicitly against the very powerful ideology of the couple as a 'team' to which even most other feminists subscribed.

The National Insurance Bill became law without taking into account the arguments of the feminists. Clearly they were fighting against a tide which wanted better social provisions for working people irrespective of the inequities which were perpetuated by the scheme. For many it was much better than nothing and the feminists were unable to persuade enough people that, while for men it was better than the existing provision, for women it did very little to really improve their material position. Women remained dependent on men and if their marriages or relationships broke down there was no reasonable scheme to help them. The objectionable separation allowance was dropped because of the difficulty of proving that a wife was innocent enough of matrimonial fault to deserve it, so such women, whose husbands did not/could not support them were forced onto National Assistance. It took a long time for this vulnerability of married women to be recognised and even now that it is, feminists are still having to fight against national insurance legislation which forces women to be dependent on their husbands.

Although it has been argued here that the feminist 'movement' in the 1940s and 1950s was not a particularly radical movement it is possible to find instances of surprising radicalism. The Women's Cooperative Guild is an example because before the Second World War, at a time when birth control was still taboo, they were arguing for abortion on demand. Equally radical during the 1940s, was the Women's Freedom League's demand for 'wages for housework'. The following extract from the Minutes of a meeting on 6 September 1943, reveals briefly not only the argument for such a policy but also the arguments against it. The argument for is very much an extension of the family allowance argument put forward by Eleanor Rathbone, and it is worth mentioning here because of the way in which this debate prefigures later discussions between feminists over the demand for 'wages' for women who stay in the home doing domestic labour.

SAQ Make a note of the arguments for and against this proposal, so that you will be able to compare them with those of later feminists in Unit 4.

The Economic Status of the Housewife

At the Discussion Meeting held on July 23rd at 8 Manchester Square, with Miss Pearson in the Chair, Mrs. Billington Greig (WFL) opened the discussion, stating that the views she was putting forward rested on the general premise that all work should be assessed on its value to the community, and the national wealth be shared by every member of that community. The community should recognise the work of the housewife and mother as a form of social service and should recompense her for it. Already in its own interest the community has taken many steps to ensure good conditions in the home and this should be the last step: child allowances and payment of the housewife and mother. She considered that marriage should be legally recognised as an equal partnership, both parties sharing their means and responsibilities. *But a wife's share of her husband's earnings or income does not give her true economic independence, because it is in indirect payment through another person for the work she does.* For true economic independence the housewife must be paid direct by the community like any other earner. In return the community should have the right to demand that the housewife and mother should be trained for her job.

Mrs. Bush read a note on the Swedish Marriage Law, one of the most advanced pieces of legislation on the subject.

Miss Munro said that the Labour Party had no official policy on the question but considered that improved social services would improve the status of the housewife. She considered that payment of the housewife might militate against the freedom of women's economic choice. Personal earnings by women from which to contribute to the upkeep of the home and meet their own expenses has been the only satisfactory solution up to now.

Miss Reeves said that the Liberal Party also had no official policy except family allowances and better social services. She felt it would create a grievance the wife and housekeeper were paid by the community while there could be no such payment for other houskeepers. Direct wage-earnings through professional and other work seems the best way of securing independence for the married woman.

Miss Frances spoke of the Married Women's Association policy of the right of a wife to a share in the family income and gave examples of hard cases under existing conditions.

Miss Pierotti said that Mrs. Billington Greig was referring rather to the economic position of the *mother* than of the housewife. *Payment by the community would probably lead to women being held in the "job" of marriage,* and also to reduced contribution by the husband towards household expenses. What was needed was to educate women to understand what their status ought to be.

Mrs. Spiller asked "What is economic independence?" He who pays the piper calls the tune and if the State pays the housewife it will hold the woman in the home and limit her freedom in other work. She felt that women need security like everyone else and should get insurance benefits in need, sickness and old age like all other citizens. Children's allowance might relieve the mother from some financial anxiety but would not increase her personal economic independence. Improved housing and social services should free the housewife and mother to undertake paid work, either whole or part time, as this alone would enable her to develop her personality fully and contribute freely to the life of the community in which she lives.

(Women's Freedom League, 1943b, emphasis added)

This discussion focuses conflicting feminist views on how the economic independence of married women could be achieved. The argument for the state's payment of married women is seen as containing the risk of women being forced to stay at home, thus reducing their opportunities for being independent wage earners.

Although they disagree about the nature of the marriage 'partnership', all the contributions we have considered here share a common view about the position of the married woman within it — that she has no economic independence. The opposition to Beveridge is thus not anti-welfare, but focuses on its failure to be 'universal' by its exemption of married women. This is identified as a lost opportunity for the state to help create greater economic independence by treating married women as individuals in their own right.

These groups accept the Beveridge framework for welfare provision, but argue that it should be extended to married women so that it becomes truly national. In this way, the discussions of welfare reflect the broader character of feminism in this period, with its commitment to improving the status of women and women's work within the home.

5 LAISSEZ-FAIRE IDEOLOGY

5.1 LAISSEZ-FAIRE AND THE '1945' CONSENSUS

The construction of the post-war welfare state between 1944 and 1948 is often treated as a period of social and political 'consensus' — particularly in the form of cross party agreement on the commitment to welfare. While there is some truth in this description, we need to be careful not to mistake consensus for the complete disappearance of disagreement and ideological conflict. The acceptance of an expanded welfare state was not achieved without conflict, and opposing voices were to be heard.

The Conservative Party itself was divided by the Beveridge proposals. It won the support of some younger Conservatives like MacMillan and Butler, who had, during the 1930s, become convinced of the need for social reform. In 1938, MacMillan had written:

The fixing of a minimum standard of life must not be regarded as merely humanitarian. It is closely related to the whole question of economic stability. There is a clear relationship between the purchasing power in the hands of the people and the demand for consumers' goods. There is an obvious relationship between the demand for consumers' goods and the level of employment among workers engaged in producing those goods.

(p. 188)

Although this 'enlightened' conservatism was to dominate the party's politics in the 1950s and the 1960s, the issue of reform was less clear cut at the end of the war.

Churchill at first resisted the implementation of Beveridge's proposals, only coming to a rather grudging acceptance of them when confronted with evidence of the degree of popular support which they commanded (and which he, correctly, feared might be captured by the Labour Party). A small group of Conservative MPs together with various employers' organizations, the private insurance companies and the BMA maintained a longer resistance to this expansion of welfare.

However, the most substantial ideological opposition was to be found among writers who tried to resist what they saw as the further encroachment of 'collectivism' on a market society. They warned of the dangers of extending the temporary war-time powers of state control into the 'normal' life of peacetime society. Lionel Robbins, an economist heavily involved in war-time planning, argued for the necessity of dismantling state controls in his *The Economic Problem in Peace and War* (1947). However, the most significant voice of opposition to the expansion of the state was Friedrick von Hayek, who published *The Road to Serfdom* in 1944. Hayek warned of the threat to liberty posed by the increasing control of society by the state, and argued that the workings of market relations were the best guarantee of individual freedom.

In the next section we focus on Hayek not simply because of his significance in this period, but because of his status as mentor and 'guiding light' for the subsequent development of laissez-faire ideology in more recent times. Hayek has come to be a revered figure for contemporary laissez-faire thinkers — identified as the 'voice in the wilderness' who warned of the coming dangers.

The lengthy extract which follows is taken from Hayek's *The Road to Serfdom* and deals with the conflict between the ideals of 'security' and 'freedom'. When reading it, try to answer the following questions.

1 What does Hayek identify as the basis of freedom?

2 What are his objections to 'security'?

3 In what ways do guarantees of security oppose freedom?

5.2 HAYEK: SECURITY AND FREEDOM

Chapter IX   Security and Freedom

> The whole of society will have become a single office and a single factory with equality of work and equality of pay.
>
> *V. I. Lenin,* 1917.

> In a country where the sole employer is the State, opposition means death by slow starvation. The old principle: who does not work shall not eat, has been replaced by a new one: who does not obey shall not eat.
>
> *L. Trotsky,* 1937.

LIKE the spurious "economic freedom", and with more justice, economic security is often represented as an indispensable condition of real liberty. In a sense this is both true and important. Independence of mind or strength of character are rarely found among those who cannot be confident that they will make their way by their own effort. Yet the idea of economic security is no less vague and ambiguous than most other terms in this field; and because of this the general approval given to the demand for security may become a danger to liberty. Indeed, when security is understood in too absolute a sense, the general striving for it, far from increasing the chances of freedom, becomes the gravest threat to it.

It will be well to contrast at the outset the two kinds of security: the limited one, which can be achieved for all, and which is therefore no privilege but a legitimate object of desire; and the absolute security which in a free

Friedrick von Hayek: spokesman of the laissez-faire opposition

society cannot be achieved for all and which ought not to be given as a privilege — except in a few special instances such as that of the judges, where complete independence is of paramount importance. These two kinds of security are, first, security against severe physical privation, the certainty of a given minimum of sustenance for all; and, secondly, the security of a given standard of life, or of the relative position which one person or group enjoys compared with others; or, as we may put it briefly, the security of a minimum income and the security of the particular income a person is thought to deserve. We shall presently see that this distinction largely coincides with the distinction between the security which can be provided for all outside of and supplementary to the market system, and the security which can be provided only for some and only by controlling or abolishing the market.

There is no reason why in a society that has reached the general level of wealth which ours has attained, the first kind of security should not be guaranteed to all without endangering general freedom. There are difficult questions about the precise standard which should thus be assured; there is particularly the important question whether those who thus rely on the community should indefinitely enjoy all the same liberties as the rest.[1] An incautious handling of these questions might well cause serious and perhaps even dangerous political problems; but there can be no doubt that some minimum of food, shelter, and clothing, sufficient to preserve health and the capacity to work, can be assured to everybody. Indeed, for a considerable part of the population of this country this sort of security has long been achieved.

Nor is there any reason why the state should not assist the individuals in providing for those common hazards of life against which, because of their uncertainty, few individuals can make adequate provision. Where, as in the case of sickness and accident, neither the desire to avoid such calamities nor the efforts to overcome their consequences are as a rule weakened by the provision of assistance, where, in short, we deal with genuinely insurable risks, the case for the state helping to organise a comprehensive system of social insurance is very strong . . . But there is no incompatibility in principle between the state providing greater security in this way and the preservation

[1] There are also serious problems of international relations which arise if mere citizenship of a country confers the right to a standard of living higher than elsewhere, and which ought not to be dismissed too lightly.

of individual freedom. To the same category belongs also the increase of security through the state rendering assistance to the victims of such "acts of God" as earthquakes and floods. Wherever communal action can mitigate disasters against which the individual can neither attempt to guard himself, nor make provision for the consequences, such communal action should undoubtedly be taken.

There is, finally, the supremely important problem of combating general fluctuations of economic activity and the recurrent waves of large-scale unemployment which accompany them. This is, of course, one of the gravest and most pressing problems of our time. But, though its solution will require much planning in the good sense, it does not — or at least need not — require that special kind of planning which according to its advocates is to replace the market. Many economists hope indeed that the ultimate remedy may be found in the field of monetary policy, which would involve nothing incompatible even with nineteenth-century liberalism. Others, it is true, believe that real success can be expected only from the skilful timing of public works undertaken on a very large scale. This might lead to much more serious restrictions of the competitive sphere, and in experimenting in this direction we shall have carefully to watch our step if we are to avoid making all economic activity progressively more dependent on the direction and volume of government expenditure. But this is neither the only, nor, in my opinion, the most promising way of meeting the gravest threat to economic security. In any case, the very necessary efforts to secure protection against these fluctuations do not lead to the kind of planning which constitutes such a threat to our freedom.

*   *   *   *   *

The planning for security which has such an insidious effect on liberty is that of a different kind. It is planning designed to protect individuals or groups against diminutions of their income which although in no way deserved yet in a competitive society occur daily, against losses imposing severe hardships having no moral justification yet inseparable from the competitive system. This demand for security is thus another form of the demand for just remuneration, a remuneration commensurate with the subjective merits and not with the objective results of a man's efforts. This kind of security or justice seems irreconcilable with freedom to choose one's employment.

Certainty of a given income can, however, not be given to all if any freedom in the choice of one's occupation is to be allowed. And if it is provided for some it becomes a privilege at the expense of others whose security is thereby necessarily diminished. That security of an invariable income can be provided for all only by the abolition of all freedom in the choice of one's employment is easily shown. Yet, although such a general guarantee of legitimate expectation is often regarded as the ideal to be aimed at, it is not a thing which is seriously attempted. What is constantly being done is to grant this kind of security piecemeal, to this group and to that, with the result that for those who are left out in the cold the insecurity constantly increases. No wonder that in consequence the value attached to the privilege of security constantly increases, the demand for it becomes more and more urgent, till in the end no price, not even that of liberty, appears too high . . . If we want to form a picture of what society would be like if, according to the ideal which has seduced so many socialists, it was organised as a single great factory, we have to look to ancient Sparta, or to contemporary Germany, which after moving for two or three generations in this direction, has now so nearly reached it.

*   *   *   *   *

In a society used to freedom it is unlikely that many people would be ready deliberately to purchase security at this price. But the policies which are now followed everywhere, which hand out the privilege of security, now to this group and now to that, are nevertheless rapidly creating conditions in which the striving for security tends to become stronger than the love of freedom. The reason for this is that with every grant of complete security to one group the insecurity of the rest necessarily increases. If you guarantee to some a fixed part of a variable cake, the share left to the rest is bound to fluctuate proportionally more than the size of the whole. And the essential element of security which the competitive system offers, the great variety of opportunities, is more and more reduced.

Within the market system, security can be granted to particular groups only by the kind of planning known as restrictionism (which includes, however, almost all the planning which is actually practised!). "Control", i.e. limitation of output so that prices will secure an "adequate" return, is the only way in which in a market economy producers can be guaranteed a certain income. But this necessarily involves a reduction of opportunities open to others. If the producer, be he entrepreneur or worker, is to be protected against underbidding by outsiders, it means that others who are worse off are precluded from sharing in the relatively greater prosperity of the controlled industries. Every restriction on the freedom of entry into a trade reduces the security of all those outside it . . . There can be little doubt that it is largely a consequence of the striving for security by these means in the last decades that unemployment and thus insecurity for large sections of the population has so much increased . . .

Thus, the more we try to provide full security by interfering with the market system, the greater the insecurity becomes; and, what is worse, the greater becomes the contrast between the security of those to whom it is granted as a privilege and the ever-increasing insecurity of the under-privileged.

*　　*　　*　　*　　*

The general endeavour to achieve security by restrictive measures, tolerated or supported by the state, has in the course of time produced a progressive transformation of society — a transformation in which, as in so many other ways, Germany has led and the other countries have followed. This development has been hastened by another effect of socialist teaching, the deliberate disparagement of all activities involving economic risk and the moral opprobrium cast on the gains which make risks worth taking but which only few can win. We cannot blame our young men when they prefer the safe, salaried position to the risk of enterprise after they have heard from their earliest youth the former described as the superior, more unselfish and disinterested occupation. The younger generation of to-day has grown up in a world in which in school and press the spirit of commercial enterprise has been represented as disreputable and the making of profit as immoral, where to employ a hundred people is represented as exploitation but to command the same number as honourable. Older people may regard this as an exaggeration of the present state of affairs, but the daily experience of the University teacher leaves little doubt that as a result of anti-capitalist propaganda values have already altered far in advance of the change in institutions which has yet taken place in this country. The question is whether by changing our institutions to satisfy the new demands, we shall not unwittingly destroy values which we still rate higher.

The change in the structure of society involved in the victory of the ideal of security over that of independence cannot be better illustrated than by a comparison of what ten or twenty years ago could still be regarded as the English and the German type of society. However great the influence of the army may have been in the latter country, it is a grave mistake to ascribe what the Englishman regarded as the "military" character of German society mainly to that influence. The difference went much deeper than could be explained on that ground, and the peculiar attributes of German society existed no less in circles in which the properly military influence was negligible than in those in which it was strong. It was not so much that at almost all times a larger part of the German people was organised for war than was true in other countries, but that the same type of organisation was employed for so many other purposes, which gave German society its peculiar character. It was that a larger part of the civil life of Germany than of any other country was deliberately organised from the top, that so large a proportion of her people did not regard themselves as independent but as appointed functionaries, which gave her social structure its peculiar character. Germany had, as the Germans themselves boasted, for long been a *Beamtenstaat* in which not only in the Civil Service proper but in almost all spheres of life income and status were assigned and guaranteed by some authority.

While it is doubtful whether the spirit of freedom can anywhere be extirpated by force, it is not certain that any people would successfully withstand the process by which it was slowly smothered in Germany. Where distinction and rank is achieved almost exclusively by becoming a salaried servant of the state, where to do one's assigned duty is regarded as more laudable than to choose one's own field of usefulness, where all pursuits that do not give a recognised place in the official hierarchy or a claim to a fixed income are regarded as inferior and even somewhat disreputable, it is too much to expect that many will long prefer freedom to security. And where the alternative to security in a dependent position is a most precarious position, in which one is despised alike for success and for failure, only few will resist the temptation of safety at the price of freedom. Once things have gone so far, liberty indeed becomes almost a mockery, since it can be purchased only by the sacrifice of most of the good things of this earth. In this state it is little surprising that more and more people should come to feel that without economic security liberty is "not worth having' and that they are willing to sacrifice their liberty for security. But it is disquieting to find Professor Harold Laski in this country employing the very same argument which has perhaps done more than any other to induce the German people to sacrifice their liberty.[1]

There can be no question that adequate security against severe privation, and the reduction of the avoidable causes of misdirected effort and consequent disappointment, will have to be one of the main goals of policy. But if these endeavours are to be successful and not to destroy individual freedom, security must be provided outside the market and competition be left to function unobstructed. Some security is essential if freedom is to be preserved, because most men are willing to bear the risk which freedom inevitably involves only so long as that risk is not too great. But while this is a truth of which we must never lose sight, nothing is more fatal than the present fashion among intellectual leaders of extolling security at the expense of freedom. It is essential that we should re-learn frankly to face the fact that freedom can only be had at a price and that as individuals we must be prepared to make severe material sacrifices to preserve our liberty. If we want to retain this we must regain the conviction on which the rule of liberty in the Anglo-Saxon countries has been based and which Benjamin Franklin expressed in a phrase applicable to us in our lives as individuals no less than as nations: "Those who would give up essential liberty to purchase a little temporary safety deserve neither liberty nor safety."

(Hayek, 1944, Chapter 9)

[1]H. J. Laski, *Liberty in the Modern State* (Pelican edition 1937, p. 51): "Those who know the normal life of the poor, its haunting sense of impending disaster, its fitful search for beauty which perpetually eludes, will realise well enough that, without economic security, liberty is not worth having."

5.3 INDIVIDUALISM AND COLLECTIVISM

The question of freedom is a recurrent theme in laissez-faire ideology, and was particularly visible in writings about the dangers of collectivism at the end of the war. Here is a brief extract from Lionel Robbins' reflections on the opposition between collectivism and individualism:

> But, beyond all this, I must confess to great fears regarding personal liberty under collectivism. Perhaps I have got things out of perspective. But I cannot get out of my head the conviction that there can be precious little freedom, precious little safeguard against arbitrary power, precious little spice and variety, in a society in which there is only one employer and only one property owner . . . I think, too, of my life as a public servant. I had an almost uniquely fortunate position, with friendly ministers, the best chief in the world, good colleagues and opportunities of liberty and initative which can have been the privilege of very few. But I have to recognize that I was seldom unconscious of that sense of unfreedom which comes from the knowledge that, if you fall out with your masters, there is no alternative way of doing what you want to do. I admire more than I can say that priestly caste, the administrative grade of the British Civil Service, whose anonymous self-sacrifice and devotion does so much to preserve order and efficiency in an otherwise disorderly scene. But I think that something quite essential would have gone out of life if we were all to become public servants in peace-time. I should fear this state of affairs as it would bear on the private life of the individual. I should fear, too, the consequences to political and cultural freedom.
>
> For these reasons and for many others which I have not time here to relate, I am still inclined to hold that the goal of progress lies in a direction different from that of over-all collectivism. I am no foe to experiment; and I recognize that there are some fields where collectivist ownership and enterprise may have important functions to perform. But, as a general principle of organization, I prefer the diffused initiative and quasi-automatism which go, or can be made to go, with private property and the market. I believe that the loose institutions of individualism offer scope for the development of a way of life, more congenial to what most of us desire in our hearts, than the tight centralized controls which are necessary if these institutions are greatly curtailed or suspended.

(Robbins, 1947, pp. 80-81)

SAQ What institutions does Robbins identify as maintaining individual freedom?

5.4 QUESTIONS AND ANSWERS

In some ways, the extracts from the proponents of market freedom may seem rather distant from our main questions about welfare and the state. They do not address particular issues of welfare provision — the Beveridge Report is nowhere mentioned. Perhaps this reflects the lack of impact of laissez-faire ideology on the debate about welfare in the post-war period. But their observations about freedom and collectivism are not without significance. Let's consider the questions which we suggested ideologies of welfare address. We have provided space for you to note down your answers before giving ours.

1   What is their idea of the state?

The state is a *danger*. Its attempts to control and direct society (either by being the sole employer or by providing guarantees of security) are a threat to individual choice and freedom. The state is the agency of collectivism and is opposed to the market which is the agency of individualism.

---

2   What do they see as the effects of welfare provisions?

Hayek sees some provision of minimum security as reasonable, but warns against its extension into guarantees which inhibit market forces and the choices which they allow individuals to make. No particular welfare provisions are identified.

---

3   What welfare should be provided?

'Security' (in Hayek's phrase) can be provided over 'common hazards of life' which are unforeseeable (sickness and accident) and 'acts of God' (earthquakes and flood). More questionable is the case of large scale unemployment — Hayek holds open the possibility of regulation through monetary policy rather than the provision of public works. The limit of 'guarantees' is to be found where the guarantee would interfere with the normal workings of the market (e.g. in the case of *income* guarantees).

---

4   What causes are seen as necessitating welfare provision?

The main distinction made by Hayek is that of 'natural disaster' (either individual or collective) and situations where choices can be made (e.g. employment and income). For the former, welfare should be provided, but not for the latter.

5   In what form should welfare be provided?

Hayek accepts that guarantees of security can be provided through the state (rather than through 'private' or 'market' mechanisms), but he emphasizes the principle of *insurance* rather than (for example) non-contributory schemes paid out of taxation.

6   What is said about the relation between welfare and the family?

Nothing. The focus is on the individual and individual circumstances and choices. But there is an assumption that the individual is economically active and not outside the labour market.

One final point can usefully be made about laissez-faire ideology in this period. One of the purposes of ideologies is to win support, and one means of doing this is to address other themes and issues of the time and *connect* them to the ideological position. Both of our extracts demonstrate this work of connection — they link laissez-faire to significant contemporary themes and issues. In reading Robbins' extract, for example, it is important to remember that one of the main themes of the war was precisely the defence of freedom against fascism, and Robbins identifies freedom with individualism. Other themes of British society's approach to the war (the need for social reconstruction, for example) which do not fit so easily are submerged. The point is perhaps most clearly made in Hayek's identification of the dangers of 'security' with the organization of German society. These are powerful ideological symbols being used within the argument about freedom.

6 '1945': SOME CONCLUSIONS?

By focusing on the different ideologies in this unit, we have to some extent overemphasised conflict about the Beveridge proposals and underplayed the degree of agreement which they created. Above all else, it must be remembered that these reforms, together with the commitment to Keynesian techniques of economic management, dominated the political field of post-war Britain. However, even within the range of different ideologies which we considered, it is possible to see how Beveridge's report constructed a major starting point for debate, and commanded some degree of support.

'The resolution is passed': a factory meeting votes for the Beveridge Report

The Fabians were, not surprisingly, strongest in their support for the Beveridge plan. Not surprisingly, because Beveridge himself had always been strongly influenced by the Fabian approach to welfare, and because the report itself was very close to Fabian proposals for reform. They were united in their appraisal of the need to create universal basic provisions, and in the commitment to the extension and strengthening of the state's responsibilities and powers. To this, the Fabians added their characteristic concern with the nature of welfare staffing — a focus on the quality and expertise of welfare administration.

For **the Socialists,** the Beveridge plan was an issue for division. For some, it represented a progressive step which, if enacted, would begin the transformation of British society towards a more just social order. For them, the key issue was to bring the Beveridge report into reality, for they were suspicious of the reluctance of the Conservatives and economic vested interests. Other socialists however, viewed the programme of reform itself with distrust. They argued that the reforms failed to touch the essential structure of inequality, and also that they represented an attempt to contain and manage opposition to British capitalism. One particular argument, as we saw, focused on the way in which the payment of family allowances (the shadow of Rathbone's endowment of motherhood scheme) would be used to reduce the level of male wages.

Feminist responses to the proposals were mixed, combining support for their general principles with fierce criticism of their uneven application in practice. In particular, they identified the failure of the plan to be truly universal, by its unequal treatment of married women. They pointed to the ways in which, at key points, the proposals excluded or reduced the benefits for married women on the basis of their presumed dependency on their husbands. For the feminists it was this failure to treat married women as independent which undermined the report's rhetoric of universality.

For the ideologists of **laissez-faire**, this was a difficult time. The experiences of state management and collective zeal during the war, together with the memory of the effects of 'unfettered capitalism' in the 1930s, had seriously undermined the popular appeal of laissez-faire arguments. Although such arguments continued to provide an expression for particular economic interests opposed to state expansion (for example, the insurance companies faced with losing their business to a state scheme), for the most part laissez-faire ideology was reduced to dire warnings about the consequences of state expansion. These warnings focused on the undermining of individual freedom and initiative which state welfare might bring about, and the danger posed by the expanded powers and controls that a larger state bureaucracy would possess over the individual citizen.

As we shall see, these various criticisms of Beveridge and welfare reform did not disappear. But for the next thirty years they persisted outside the mainstream of political and welfare debate, returning in new forms and with greater visibility with the crisis of welfare in the mid-1970s.

REFERENCES

ABBOTT, E. and BOMPAS, K. (1943) *The Woman Citizen and Social Security: A Criticism of the Proposals Made in the Beveridge Report as they Affect Women,* London, Mrs Bompas.

ADDISON, P. (1977) *The Road to 1945,* London, Quartet.

BEVERIDGE, W. (1942) *Social Insurance and Allied Services,* Cmnd 6404, London, HMSO.

BEVERIDGE, W. (1944) *Full Employment in A Free Society,* London, Allen and Unwin.

BIRMINGHAM FEMINIST HISTORY GROUP (1979) 'Feminism as femininity?', *Feminist Review* No. 3.

CLARKE, J. S. (1943) 'The staff problem', in ROBSON, W. A. (ed.) *Social Security,* London, Allen and Unwin.

GRIFFITHS, J. (1969) *Pages from Memory,* London, Dent.

HAYEK, F. A. (1944) *The Road to Serfdom,* 1962 edn, London, Routledge and Kegan Paul.

HILL, D. (ed.) (1977) *Tribune 40,* Extract from *Tribune* editorial of 4 December 1942, London, Quartet.

MACMILLAN, H. (1938) *The Middle Way,* London, Macmillan.

MISHRA, R. (1981) *Society and Social Policy,* (2nd edn), London, Macmillan.

ROBBINS, L. (1947) *The Economic Problem in Peace and War,* London, Macmillan.

ROBSON, W. A. (ed.) (1943) *Social Security,* Preface, London, Allen and Unwin.

SOCIALIST PARTY OF GT BRITAIN (undated) *Family Allowances — A Socialist Analysis,* London, SPGB.

WILSON, E. (1980) *Halfway to Paradise,* London, Methuen.

WOMEN'S FREEDOM LEAGUE (1943a) 'The Beveridge Report', *The Women's Bulletin* No. 285, 29 January.

WOMEN'S FREEDOM LEAGUE (1943b) 'The economic status of the housewife', *The Women's Bulletin,* 6 September.

ACKNOWLEDGEMENTS

Grateful acknowledgement is made to the following sources for material used in this unit:

Text

HMSO for W. Beveridge, *Social Insurance and Allied Services,* Cmnd 6404, 1942, reprinted by permission of HMSO; George Allen and Unwin and Fabian Society for W. A. Robson, *Social Security,* 1943; Harold Griffiths for J. Griffiths, *Pages from Memory,* Dent; The Socialist Party of Great Britain for *Family Allowances – A Socialist Analysis,* n.d.; *Tribune* for 'Editorial, 4 December, 1942' ed. D. Hill; Fawcett Library for E. Abbott and K. Bompas, *The Woman Citizen and Social Security,* Women's Freedom League, 1943; Routledge and Kegan Paul and University of Chicago Press for F. A. Hayek, *The Road to Serfdom,* 1962.

Illustrations

p. 50 John Topham; *p. 55* London Express News and Features; *pp. 60 and 85* BBC Hulton Picture Library; *p. 78* Jacques Haillol/Camera Press.

UNIT 4

IDEOLOGIES OF WELFARE: INTO THE 1980s

Prepared for the Course Team by Carol Smart, John Clarke and Allan Cochrane

CONTENTS

INTRODUCTION

You will remember that Unit 1 began by examining how the consensus about the welfare state was broken in the mid-1970s. In this unit, you will be able to examine some of the consequences of this break-up. The attack by the new conservatism (sometimes called 'neo-liberalism') revived some of the themes of laissez-faire ideology in its condemnation of the excesses of state intervention. The warnings of Friedrich von Hayek about the 'road to serfdom' were, it seemed, finally being heeded.

However, as Unit 1 indicated, the successes and failures of the 1945 welfare state were not only being re-evaluated by this new conservatism. As you will see in the course of this unit, other criticisms of welfare provision and other programmes for reorganizing welfare have developed from the late seventies into the eighties which lead in very different directions from that of laissez-faire ideology.

It is the arguments presented here (and others like them) which command the possible futures for the welfare state in Britain.

1 LAISSEZ-FAIRE AND CONTEMPORARY WELFARE

Although laissez-faire was marginal to the debates about welfare and post-war reconstruction, and remained outside the main political debates about welfare in the 1950s and 1960s, it was never to disappear completely during this period. Its revival and political flourishing in the Conservative Party in the 1970s drew on an established intellectual basis in an organization called the Institute of Economic Affairs. Founded in 1957, the IEA sponsored economic analysis and published a variety of books, reports and pamphlets maintaining the importance of the free market and criticizing the growth of state powers and spending. Professor Hayek (whom you will remember from Unit 3) has been one of the main intellectual mentors of the IEA, and a frequent contributor to its publications.

1.1 MONETARISM AND STATE SPENDING

While in Britain the IEA and other economic commentators continued to explore the basis of freedom in market relations and 'consumer sovereignty', a similar analysis was being constructed by American economists, best known in the work of Milton Friedman. Here too, one central focus was on the economic and social consequences of increased government spending and the inefficiencies of state provision. The Friedman position identified a number of failings in the welfare state:

1   It is self interest which normally guides us in spending money, but those spending 'welfare money' have no incentive not to be inefficient and wasteful.

2   In contrast self interest on the part of welfare bureaucrats will lead them to direct money to themselves, either in the form of corruption or empire-building.

3   Spending money on others involves the imposition of control. It makes those who receive welfare benefits dependent and incapable of making their own decisions.

4   The welfare state depends on 'the use of force', where the state takes the individual's money in taxation. It is, thus, a threat to freedom.

At the core of the Friedman argument, however, was the proposition that the expansion of public spending which accompanied the welfare state had a damaging effect on economic performance. Public spending threatened or held back the proper development of the wealth producing private sector. One of the strongest adherents of the Friedman argument, Sir Keith Joseph, provides our first extract. In this extract, he links the arguments about public and private sectors to the theory of state intervention argued for by Friedman and others. 'Monetarism', as it has become known, argued that the state should not intervene directly in economic management, but should limit itself to indirect management through controlling the money supply. (You may remember this policy was mentioned by Hayek, in Unit 3, p. 79.)

SAQ   What does Joseph argue is the need for reducing public spending?

Sir Keith Joseph: 'monetarism is not enough'

Cuts in state spending are essential both to make way for the revival of the wealth-creating sector and to achieve a deceleration of the growth of the money supply. Cuts in state spending of sufficient magnitude to reduce inflation substantially will require strong nerves. But the alternative would be accelerating decline in standard of living and in employment within the next few years.

   To hold down the growth of the money supply to a level commensurate with the expected growth in productive capacity, and to keep it there, is part of the cure for inflation.[1] If the whole economy were private, then all firms would be subject to the resulting constriction — and only the unsound would need to go. But the whole economy is not private. Nearly two-thirds is statist, and insensitive in itself to contraction of the money supply. It is fed with

[1]*Crisis '75 . . . ?* Sir John Hicks and others. Occasional Paper 43. Institute of Economic Affairs, 1975. In particular the essay 'Turning Point or Moment of Danger?', E. Victor Morgan.

money which is expanded automatically to maintain given levels of expenditure in real terms — 'funny money', as Samuel Brittan calls it. Indeed, while money supply is contracting, budgetary spending is expanding.

So the state sector bids up interest rates, bids off funds, bids away manpower and leaves the force of the monetary contraction focussed on the private sector. While the activity rate is low, and stocks have run down, as now, the private sector feels the pinch of lower demand and increased costs but, though there are record levels of bankruptcies, the sector as a whole can temporarily increase its liquidity . . .

In other words, the monetary process is both a cause of inflation and a link in a wider chain of cause and effect Monetary contraction in a mixed economy strangles the private sector unless the state sector contracts with it and reduces its take from the national income.

Hence my title 'Monetarism is Not Enough'. Detaxing and the restoration of bold incentives and encouragements to business and industry are necessary too. Until the state contracts, and indeed until enterprise is encouraged both by this contraction together with some assurance that it will stay contracted, and by less destructive taxation and intervention, there will not be the confidence nor the climate for entrepreneurship and risk-taking that will alone secure prosperity, high employment and economic health.

Cuts mean cuts. At present, we have learned, actual government expenditure has outrun projected by several percent of the GNP. We shall need to cut it back by several percent. Pseudo-cuts of future programmes will not be enough. We shall need to cut state employment and subsidies to rail, steel, housing and the supported sector. We shall need to explain that subsidised employment is not really saving jobs because the subsidies have to be paid for and the paying for them loses more jobs than are saved. We must demonstrate that state spending — including subsidies — is a cause of many smaller firms cutting their labour force or going out of business . . .

Our monetary problems reflect the underlying weakness of this man-made chaos, the divorce of work from production, of cost from benefit, of reward from performance, the greatest government spending spree of all time which is designed primarily to keep people busy instead of useful . . .

This is going through the motions, keeping up appearances, window dressing a fraudulent facade. Behind the facade, the private sector that produces the goods which people want is restricted by controls, over-taxed by local and central government and harassed by officials. Our monetary arrangements are bound to reflect this dichotomy. Hence the public sector's 'funny money', which, we now learn belatedly, has led to massive state over-spending, while the ever more constricted wealth-producing sector has to conduct its accounts, taxes and dividends in terms of an increasingly threadbare pound . . .

Monetarism is not enough. This is not intended as a counsel of despair, but a warning note. Government's intention to contract the money supply is welcome and potentially beneficial to all. But it is not enough unless there is also the essential reduction of the state sector and the essential encouragement of enterprise. We are over-governed, over-spent, over-taxed, over-borrowed and over-manned. If we shirk the cure, the after-effects of continued over-taxation will be worse than anything we have endured hitherto. Our ability to distinguish between economic reality and economic make-believe will decline further. We shall experience accelerated worsening of job prospects, the growing flight of those with professional skills, talent and ability to other countries, and an increase in the shabbiness and squalor of everyday lives.

That is why, by itself, the strict and unflinching control of money supply though essential is not enough. We must also have substantial cuts in tax and public spending and bold incentives and encouragements to the wealth creators, without whose renewed efforts we shall all grow poorer.

(Joseph, 1977)

Joseph seems to be arguing that although monetarism (the control of money supply by the government) is a crucial aspect of economic policy, it must be supplemented by a serious reduction in public spending. There are three connected reasons for this policy: first, it is the 'private' sector which is wealth producing; second, the private sector has been restricted by excessive government regulation and excessive taxation; third, this taxation has been used to pay for an expanding, inefficient and unproductive public sector. This distinction between private and public sectors is central to new laissez-faire thinking, and it plays a key role in their analysis of welfare.

1.2 LAISSEZ-FAIRE AND ANTI-STATISM

But the attack on welfare spending from this revived laissez-faire position was never solely restricted to questions of its cost. The question of financing was always linked to a much wider questioning of whether the existing state provision was the best way of providing welfare. In a pamphlet called *Breaking the Spell of the Welfare State,* three authors from the Social Affairs Unit of the Centre for Policy Studies (established by Sir Keith Joseph in 1974) argued that the welfare state had become impervious to criticism. They argued that the need for serious thinking about welfare was being impeded by the 'spell' of the welfare state. This extract from the pamphlet offers nine reasons for the power of this 'spell' of welfare.

The spell of the welfare state: nine aspects

1. The welfare state is perceived as normal. Nationalised welfare is part of the establishment. Though some of its departments have a relatively short history, their functions are perceived as permanent. (Departments of course often disappear in re-organisation). Though we managed without the welfare state for most of our history, we cannot *think* of life without it now . . . The once-new institutions become tied to others in the system in a complex of departmental relations, accretions, mutual interests, legitimising each other, so that any change in one thing means a hundred other changes.

2. The welfare state is perceived as safe and free. To change what is natural, what we are used to, is risky. This is not a case of the devil one knows being better than the devil one does not know because the separation of payment and service prevents us knowing the devil we have. Riboud has argued that if only workers knew in a graphic way say, on their pay slips, where their taxes were going, there would be pressure for fundamental change. Certainly at the other end of the chain many of the well-intentioned staff in schools, colleges, and local authority offices do imagine that they are paid by the local authority. It says so on *their* pay slips. The way that the welfare state is funded does not only have consequences for its efficiency but also for its public image. It is seen as a provider of services not a robber of the poor, as people giving services not as people living off productive workers; as distributing benefits not as preventing that money being used for industrial investment. Even private enterprise, which is so vocal about government spending in general and which pays so much of the welfare *bill,* has often failed to take as critical an interest in welfare *expenditure.*

3. The beneficiaries of the welfare state will argue for it. The welfare state provides many people with their livelihood. Many people depend on it directly for their income: teachers, lecturers, social workers, environmental health officers, youth workers, race relations officials, Manpower Services Commission employees, education advisers, employees of 'voluntary' organisations in receipt of permanent grants, and bureaucrats, central and local, DHSS and DES. Then there is the secondary welfare industry: academics who research the welfare state, publishers who sell to welfare state students, journalists who write for welfare state papers, TV and media men who 'document' the welfare state. For some of these the welfare state provides a convenient stable income. For others life would be very cold outside it. Abusive though they may be, terms such as 'Poverty Lobby' and 'Race Relations Industry' do draw attention to the financial stake welfarists have in the perpetuations of the welfare state. It is one that few electioneering politicians can afford to neglect. The welfare state is another estate — a power bloc. It is not just the recipient of tax payers' money but is an *active* lobby in the land through its syndicates, through civil servants and at local government level. It is a 'new class' with its own class interest . . .

4. *Those who research and evaluate the welfare state are 'insiders'.* The welfare state is not, generally accountable through the market. It is true that some of its products are difficult to hide (the illiterate teenager, for example) and some of its organisations do simulate aspects of the market (as in limited parental choice of schools). But accountability to the customer is chiefly through committees and the ballot box. The latter gives a very limited and occasional choice when compared to market choice. The day to day running and evaluation of the welfare state is carried out by its own members and much of this autonomy is filtered down the service 'out of professional deference', so that most headmasters, for instance, have considerable autonomy in their schools and teachers in their class. It is the combination of this 'professional' autonomy with lack of customer choice, reinforced by syndicalist obstruction, invisible costs, bureaucracy and rhetoric that makes the welfare state so unaccountable. Moreover there are intensified problems when professional autonomy is given to personnel like teachers and social workers whose professionalism is limited, under-developed and sometimes non-existent. The welfare state is not *externally* accountable.

5. *Privately admitted truths about the welfare state are denied in public.* Vested corporate interest leads to the phenomenon of 'open secrets'. The researchers' problem with the welfare state is not getting to *know* what goes on in this or that department. It is, rather, *showing* it to be the case. There is no problem finding teachers who will reveal abuses and extravagancies in schools. At the drop of a gin they will go further than any outside critic in their tales of futility and extravagance. But there is the world of difference between what individual employees of the welfare state will say in private and what their association secretaries say at the Blackpool Annual Conference. It is of the nature of failure, inefficiency, extravagance and the rest that they are difficult to research . . .

6. *The welfare state influences the words used to criticise it.* Marxist scholars have, for their purposes, recently devoted much attention to the role of cultural factors in preserving dominant capitalist institutions. In the same way the critic who would enter the welfare debate soon finds that cultural aspects of the welfare state help sustain its 'dominance'. Language is the chief of these cultural aspects. The debate is soggy with loose talk about 'compassion', 'caring professions', 'need', 'the importance of trying to do something' and so on. Critics can be discredited by accusations of 'not caring'.

Appeals to sentiment (not morality since the talk is too loose for that) combine with other vocabularies, such as that of expertise. Members of the welfare state award themselves titles and qualifications which emphasise their knowledge. The job advertisements in *New Society* and *Social Work Today* display a joyous feast of imperialistic titles. With the help of a little Marxist folklore these languages can be mobilised into moral tales, in pay claims, for example, — the NUT fights not for itself, but for the 'needs' of 'children' and the 'right' of 'all' to a decent education. The cuts have produced the supreme occasion for mobilising language in this way. The world has been re-ordered in heroic fable fashion, with 'those in need' being 'attacked' by the 'heartless cuts' of a 'vicious' Tory government, while the allies of the 'needy' the 'caring professions' in collaboration with NALGO, pledge themselves to 'fight to defend the rights' and so on. It is odd that these people who see landlords as 'unscrupulous', public schools as 'élitist', and who make use of the other cardboard characters of the fable are the foremost in the attack on other people's use of stereotypes.

7. *Being an employee of the welfare state is more honourable than being a critic.* Despite copious rewards, job security, pensions and autonomy, welfarists manage to convince non-welfarists that they have some sort of special claim to altruism. Certainly it is not difficult for them to claim, in seeking to counter the critic's arguments, that they 'are at least trying to help people with their problems' while he is 'just being destructive'. The idea that action is constructive even when it is ineffective, harmful or expensive and that destructive criticism is to be deplored even when it saves money and stops harm is an odd one in any circumstance. But in the context of the welfare state it strains belief beyond the normal limits. For the lessons of the last twenty years have been that it is far easier to start up or extend a welfare state activity than to reduce or abolish one that already exists. Effective destructive criticism turns out to be a rare, valuable and difficult exercise . . .

8. *The critic is denied the information necessary for criticism.* Much information necessary for the criticism of the welfare state belongs to it and it guards it jealously: witness the dispute about publishing school examination success rates. In other cases the welfare state does not keep the records that would make effective criticism possible as the case of the 'Forgotten Children' showed. A mixture of these two sorts of problems plus that of 'open secrets' would present powerful obstacles to two crucial and necessary research operations. The first is that of establishing the administrative costs of the NHS. The second is that of finding the real costs, student numbers and staff-student ratios in higher education.

But the most crucial kind of information which the welfarists hide relates to the criteria for their own dissolution. It really is a waste of time for the critic to pile statistic upon statistic, classroom observation upon classroom observation, survey upon survey and argument upon argument, all in order, to arrive at a conclusion that can be brushed aside as irrelevant or 'interesting'. As an essential preliminary it would be, to put it mildly, useful to get clear just what the various departments of the welfare state *would* accept as justifying the abolition of this or that activity. The same principle applies to the assessment of individual employees of the welfare state. If there is no point short of rape which the National Union of Teachers will accept as justifying the sacking of a teacher, then it is not a researcher that is needed but an agent-provocateur. Surely the first issue for the current enquiry into social work, before collecting 'evidence', is to get these 'dissolution criteria' clear and to then state them publicly.

Indeed the principle can be extended. It could be an obligation for departments of the welfare state, not only to spell out what they would accept as evidence of failure but how their subsequent action would relate to such evidence. In the unlikely event of the report of the current DHSS investigation into social work being very negative, how *big* a reduction would be undertaken? These may appear excessive concerns unless one remembers the alternative that criticism is encouraged and welcomed but is totally unrelated to service reduction or expansion . . .

The welfarists challenged this case for clarity of aims and standards by pointing out that working with people is more difficult to assess and evaluate than working, say, with cars. So it is. But the critic is surely right to expect there to be at least a minimal aim and a minimal standard, a level below which something should definitely be accepted as a failure. If that is not possible the welfare state is truly a state in anarchy. In fact, of course, more than that is possible. In day-to-day teaching and social work judgements are made by teachers, lecturers and social workers about each other's work, about desirable and undesirable courses of action. Indeed, the ethic of professionalism they claim heightens their powers of discretion, choice and priority. More mundanely, I have never seen any of them refuse promotion on the grounds that when it comes to the evaluation of staff merit it is impossible to proceed because of the standard problems that arise in 'work with people' as distinct from 'things'! . . .

Criticism can only bite on something which is explicit about aims, standards, values and criteria, and which makes these publicly available. This explains the paradox that it is easy to criticise well-run institutions and very difficult to criticise institutions with undeclared and unrelated aims, half-visible standards, poor professional development, sentimental appeal and so on. It is this paradox that makes the welfare state not only answerable for its own condition but also for the poor debate about that condition. This is surely a fascinating variation of power without accountability.

9. Finally, and most importantly the welfare state distributes the burden of proof unfairly. All the earlier discussion about the requirements of an adequate criticism in an ideal debate rests upon a rather odd 'given' assumption that it is up to the critic to prove that the welfare state is inadequate, or that one of its parts should be changed or cut, or that certain personnel should be sacked. This is clearly a ludicrous requirement to apply to the work of some independent academic or journalist critic. *It is the welfare state that consumes public money and it is its obligation to prove that it is not wasting it.* It is the welfare state that is a social experiment and it is up to its adherents to show it has not failed. Since it is the welfare state that has the resources for assessment, it is up to it to use them. The burden of proof is not on the critic but on the welfare state. It has managed to evade that obligation for over a quarter of a century but nothing (not even the licence given to the welfare state) can last for ever. The role of the critic is not to 'prove' any part of the welfare state wrong but to prick, chide and goad a self-satisfied web of self-perpetuating bureaucracy into giving an account of itself; to see that it is a radical and thorough account and to make sure it is visible, well-evidenced and in keeping with the experimental nature of the institution.

Conclusion

In the best of worlds this strategy for evaluation is not a satisfactory way to produce accountability. But, in the absence of a market and any customer choice, critical debate is essential. Even that will not work if the spell of the welfare state is not broken. If it is allowed to: hide information, appeal to sentiment and professional demarcation, be immune from incisive and sustained analysis, build up a collusive and syndicated web of vested interest, dictate the terms of any debate, award itself its own language, be persistently coy about its standards and aims, conceal its costs, present itself as free and without risk, pass itself off as normal and irreplaceable, evade the responsibility for destructive criticism, and place the burden of proof on others, then even the very limited sort of accountability provided by public debate will be destroyed.

The priorities for the critic are clear. The first priority is to point out the need for continuous scrutiny, evaluation and public debate caused by the absence of market choice. The second is to expose the threat that the spell of the welfare state poses to such evaluation and the debate and thus demystify the welfare state. The second priority will, on occasions, call for evidence, sustained criticism, closeness to practice, detail and the other qualities of adequate criticism insofar as they are practically possible. But it will also call for selectivity in examples, hyperbole, rhetoric and, on occasions, abuse, polemic and humour. Unless the spell is broken by exposure, the welfare state will rest substantially immune from criticism.

(Anderson, Lait and Marsland, 1977, pp. 23-31)

SAQ Which groups are seen as having an interest in maintaining the current structure of the welfare state, and why?

This argument about the 'self-interest' of bureaucrats and professionals in defending the existing structures of welfare is in keeping with the general themes of laissez-faire. It identifies self-interest as one of the main (if not *the* main) motive in social and economic life. The objections to state provision are partly that it creates a monopoly position for some interests (those working for the state). That monopoly means that state providers are *not accountable.* Laissez-faire writers mean something specific by this claim. It does not refer so much to *political accountability* as to economic accountability — the laws of the market. State monopoly of provision means that the laws of demand and supply — the ability of the consumer to choose — are blocked. The attack on welfare identifies one set of interests (state providers) as having the monopoly power to block other interests — 'our' interests as consumers.

1.3 LAISSEZ-FAIRE AND THE MARKET

Necessarily then, this criticism of state monopoly is linked to the proposal of an alternative vision of how welfare should be organized. This alternative stresses the need to reintroduce market relations (sometimes called 'privatization') and consumer choice into the supply of welfare.

Our next two extracts are taken from Arthur Seldon's book *Charge!* Seldon has been one of the leading members of the IEA, and *Charge!* is devoted to exploring the distinction between the public and private elements of welfare. He argues that many of what are represented as 'the public goods' of welfare are, in fact, *private goods.* They should, therefore, be provided in ways which allow the individual consumer to choose how his or her needs should be met. In our first extract, he applies this distinction to the issue of health care provision.

SAQ Why does Seldon think that the NHS is an inefficient way to deliver health care?

5 Medical care: making the payment fit the case

Few of us under forty-five remember paying for medical care directly. Yet few health services are public goods, in the sense used in this book. Preventive measures benefit everyone in the area whether they pay or not, so charging is impracticable or uneconomic, but hospital treatment is private, family doctor services are essentially personal, most local authority services are separable and personal — health centres, midwifery, health visitors, home nursing, ambulance, family planning.

There are some 'catastrophic' risks (such as major surgery or crippling diseases) against which it is very costly to insure, and people may fatalistically prefer to run the risks rather than reduce their living standards by insuring against a rare disease or an accident that may never happen. It is possible for individuals or for society as a whole to pay too much to restore health after disasters.

This reasoning may sound harsh, but it is people who ignore the 'opportunity costs' — the enormous sacrifice in education, housing, or pensions or everyday consumption required for total health — who are (unwittingly) callous. People make better judgements as individuals than in the mass. No individual man (or woman) thinks health must be secured at *all* costs: he (or she) would otherwise never cross the road, or smoke, or swim, or fly, or eat without a food taster. It is only the National Health Service — a mass, make-believe, macro-artifact — that teaches the myth that the best health can be preserved or restored 'free' for all. In practice it does not do what it preaches, it has to ration kidney machines, for example, and so condemns some patients to death . . .

In the real world there are unavoidable or accepted risks to health, and treating ill-health uses resources. The costs can mostly be covered by insurance, and people with low incomes can be enabled to insure by a reverse income tax or by having their premiums paid on a sliding scale by government, as has been done in Australia. Catastrophic risks can be collectively tax-paid, as war damage was from 1939 to 1945. Most Western industrialised countries have mixtures of social and private, compulsory and voluntary, insurance. The result is that they channel more resources per head to medical care than we in Britain, who for the most part (95 per cent) are allowed to pay only by taxation. In Europe, North America, Australasia 6½ to 8 per cent of the Gross National Product goes to medical care; in Britain it is barely 5½ per cent. The higher figure indicates the advantages of diversifying sources of finance. Perhaps even more important, it reflects the preferences of the people who pay. This is the reply to defenders of the British system, which relies mainly on one source, who say that resources, even if less in Britain, are used more efficiently than in other countries. The reply is that, whatever the relative efficiency of the British state system, which is debatable, it does not allow people to pay in the ways they prefer. It is imposed on the people by politicians, officials and 'experts' who claim they know better. They have not been able to escape from it because all the political parties have supported it.

That is why we in Britain — and only we in Britain among Western industrialised countries — have a 'National Health Service'. The reason asserted for making people pay by taxes is that it removes the price barrier, so that everyone can have the treatment he 'needs' without worrying about paying. This may be the reason that moved the early enthusiasts for the NHS, like Aneurin Bevan in 1946, but it is still being repeated by his followers today, thirty years later, when social conditions have changed beyond recognition so that many can pay, directly out of pocket or by insurance, and when, in any event, the methods of dealing with poverty have been transformed and it is no longer an insurmountable barrier to medical care . . .

Rationing health care

What stands in the way of equality of access to medical care (or anything else) is inequality of income. This inequality produces unequal *demand* for medical care, and it is tempting to take the short cut of making income irrelevant and equalising the *supply* by announcing that it is available 'free' without limit to all comers. This is called abolishing 'rationing by the purse'. It has externalities: it makes politicians important and creates jobs for bureaucrats.

But it does not abolish rationing. Since there is no price to apportion supply between the various demands, there must be rationing by other means. In the National Health Service medical care is rationed above all by time. 'First come, first served' sounds fair but it favours the fleet of foot, the loud in voice. People and patients who are rich in time receive more or better medical care than those who are poor in time. The more individuals can wait and queue, the more attention or the better treatment they receive. So the work-evading worker or the self-centred housewife has better access to the National Health Service and gets more out of it than the conscientious worker or the self-less housewife. What sort of equality is that?

The other rationing devices, no less arbitrary, are influence (if you know your doctor or hospital official you are treated better than if you don't), literacy (the middle classes who speak the same language as the doctor do better than the working classes), cunning (those of any class who know how to 'work' the system do better than those who resignedly accept it), sex-attraction (which favours women), blackmail (of doctors who will not readily sign certificates), and other arbitrary influences like political status which ensures earlier treatment for Ministers than for the tax-payers they are supposed to serve.

The irony of rationing under the National Health Service, which its enthusiasts will not face, is that these differences are even more objectionable than differences in income, which at least to some degree reflect differences in value to the community. For differences in influence and bully-power are even more difficult to reduce or remove. Favouritism is more widespread in the National Health Service than we like to admit, as it is in other 'free' systems in Russia, Hungary, Poland and Bulgaria. The NHS has not abolished inequality: it has driven inequality underground and made it more difficult to correct.

Evolving a refined structure of charging
In all, a much more refined financing mechanism is required than taxation, both to minimise the deterrent effect to patients of fees or insurance costs and to use price as a reminder to them and to doctors and nurses that medical care uses scarce resources that could be applied elsewhere. Other countries such as Australia and the USA have gradually evolved and refined mixtures of voluntary and compulsory, state and private insurance, coinsurance or 'patient's fractions' (where the patient bears a proportion of charges shared with the insurer) and deductibles (where the patient bears the first slice of the charge), state assistance for low-income people to enable them to insure along with everyone else, and so on . . .

The main triumph of the mixed systems overseas is that they maximise the resources for medical care, which the NHS does not. More accurately, they approach nearer to the *optimum* amount, in the sense that they enable people to say how much they want to spend on medical care at the expense of all the other goods and services they could have. These mixed systems create no false hopes and no myths. They show what the vast range of medical services cost, and they allow people to pay in the ways they prefer. They have created no Nirvana, or mirage of 'the best medical care for everyone', which we in Britain have been misled into thinking was not only possible but what the NHS was giving us in our everyday lives, but which it has not given, does not give, and cannot ever give.

(Seldon, 1977, Chapter 5, pp. 83-90)

Seldon offers a number of arguments about the 'inefficiency' of the NHS. It suppresses individual choice about health care. It places resource allocation in the hands of bureaucrats and professionals, rather than making it responsive to 'choices'. Finally, although created to offset economic inequality, it has produced other forms of inequality in its place.

Our second extract deals with one of the central themes of recent laissez-faire arguments. It returns to the distinction we noted earlier between political accountability and economic accountability. Here Seldon argues that democratic control through present systems of political accountability provides only a very imperfect representation of public interest. In contrast, he argues that the market offers a more thorough and responsive indicator of public choice.

SAQ What arguments does Seldon provide for the superiority of the market as an indicator of public preference?

True and false measures of public preferences
In Britain there are only two ways of measuring what the public wants: in the ballot box and the market. The ballot box records votes by crosses cast for this or that party, policy or politician. The market records votes by money

paid for this or that commodity, service, brand, firm or business man.

The ballot box is crude compared with the market. The ballot box is used locally every three and nationally up to five years: the market is used every day or few days (for food, newspapers, transport, etc), every few months (clothes, books, etc) or years (furniture, homes, etc).

The ballot box says: 'This is my list of 57 varieties: take it or leave it.' The market says: 'This is my one item: pay for as much or as little as you want.' (Motto, p. 2.)

The ballot box says: 'This is what we promise.' The market says: 'What you see before your very eyes is what you take away if you pay.'

The ballot box says: 'Aren't our party slogans splendid!' The market says: 'Judge us by your experience of our product.'

The ballot box says: 'We are saints, public-spirited, selfless and honest. The others are devils, in the pay of vested interests, selfish, dishonest.' The market says: 'We are the best. Compare our value, quality, price.'

The ballot box says: 'Look! Benefits galore! All Free! 'The market says: 'All our goods are priced; tax shown separately.'

This contrast is over-simplified but basically right. Even if allowance is made for advertising, the persuasion of people to try this rather than that breakfast cereal, washing powder or newspaper is infinitely harmless contrasted with the persuasion to 'buy' this or that political slogan, promise or policy. You can, with little loss, change from one cereal, powder or paper to another every few days. But you are stuck with the wrong political policy for years or a lifetime (no matter how bad it becomes, the NHS will go on and on and on).

Although the ballot box is very much a second best to the market, it must be used for public goods because opinion on, say, how much and what quality of defence, cannot easily be measured in the market by individuals voting with their money. But even where there are private benefits, the ballot box is still used because wrong thinking brought it into being and vested interests keep it going even where it is inferior to the market.

(Seldon, 1977, Appendix 1)

Seldon argues that the market is a better indicator because prices are immediately responsive to consumer choices. By contrast elections are infrequent exercises of choice. The market offers choices between particular goods or services, while the electoral process offers only choices between promises. Consumer sovereignty — the 'free play of market forces' — remains one of the central themes of laissez-faire ideology.

Contemporary laissez-faire views of welfare centre on the idea of reducing the state's 'monopoly' of welfare provision, and offer the prospect of the state's responsibilities being cut back to providing an essential minimum. Beyond this, welfare would become a matter of individual choice exercised through market forces. This, they argue, would create a more efficient supply of welfare which would be more responsive to individual needs and choices.

By contrast, the state's present monopoly is seen as inefficient and damaging. Inefficient because it is not subject to the disciplines of competition and consumer sovereignty. Damaging because it is unproductive (of wealth), costly (to the taxpayer), and encourages dependence on the state rather than individual independence.

2 FEMINISM AND SOCIAL POLICY

Since the 1911 National Insurance Act feminists have been fully aware of the importance of state benefits to the living standards of women and their children. This recognition has been based on the undeniable empirical evidence that men frequently cannot, and often will not, support their wives and dependents. Feminists have therefore demanded benefits such as family allowances and maternity benefits to assist women when they are at their economically most vulnerable, namely when they are mothers. They have argued that it is the onset of motherhood that affects the lives of most women because their ability to earn a living wage (which is still not equal to that of men) is reduced through the demands of childcare. In consequence women, it is maintained, are forced to be dependent on a private system of benefit if they cannot earn a wage, namely so-called housekeeping money. Generations of feminists have therefore argued that housekeeping money, besides being unreliable and often unrelated to a man's wage and a family's needs, has too many strings attached to it. It introduces an economic and often psychological inequality into relationships and it gives men power over their wives and dependents.

The demand for some form of state benefits and provision is therefore a continuous ingredient of twentieth century feminism, and feminism in the 1970s and early 1980s is no exception. In fact the recognition of the vulnerability of women in the family, that so-called haven-in-a-heartless-world, and the realization that it is women who are the largest group living on, or dependent upon, inadequate state benefits has made social policy a central concern of many modern feminists. But this concern is now twofold. On the one hand feminists are determined that social welfare provision should meet the needs of women and not just men, and are consequently still engaged in a rigorous debate with the legacy of the Beveridge Plan which consigned married women to involuntary dependency. But on the other hand they are forced to defend the welfare state from disintegration and even deliberate annihilation at the hands of successive Labour and Conservative governments. Voices of criticism against the welfare state can all too easily be interpreted as reactionary or ill-timed. However contemporary feminists have refused to be marginalized in this way, because of their awareness that there is little point in struggling to preserve a system of welfare if success simply perpetuates a system of oppression of women. So feminist criticism has not abated, and the defensive battle for the principles of welfare coincides with an aggressive battle to transform the basic premiss of the current system.

2.1 FEMINISM IN THE 1970s

The Women's Liberation Movement (WLM) in the last quarter of the twentieth century has not been a simple resurrection of former feminisms. It is not solely concerned with changing state policies and challenging structural discriminations, although these struggles are very important. It has been as much to do with individual liberation as with traditional forms of political struggle. In addition to this emphasis on the personal and the private sphere as arenas for political struggle, the new feminism has rejected traditional male forms of organization. This was a grass roots movement with no leaders and no hierarchies. All women were supposed to have an equal voice and no women were supposed to become leaders of the movement. This structurelessness and the emphasis on the 'personal as political' would have been an anathema to earlier feminists who tended to organize in traditional bureaucratic ways with presidents, vice-presidents and treasurers, and tended to use figureheads to lead the movement.

The WLM is a politically autonomous movement. It is not an integrated part of the Left and it is distinct from Left policies although it does occasionally form alliances with trade unions and Left groups. Unlike suffrage organizations such as the NUWSS men cannot join the WLM. This is because no-one can *join* because it is not that sort of organization, but also because men are deliberately excluded. However, like the suffrage movement, the WLM is a heterogeneous movement which embraces a range of political beliefs and strategies. Some modern femininists disdain any alliances with men and also reject attempts to reform legislation and state provision, preferring to adopt revolutionary politics. Others feel it is necessary to engage with the Left and with trade unions and even to operate as a political lobby or pressure group if the circumstances demand it.

You will therefore be able to identify different approaches and emphases between the extracts we have selected from feminist writings. All of the extracts are written by feminists even though the organizations they represent, such as the National Council for Civil Liberties or the Claimants' Union are not expressly feminist groups. You will observe that all have one thing in common and that is that they share the political conviction that the state should provide benefits to women and that the state should work to alleviate women's dependency and poverty inside the family. They are therefore asking for an *extension* of the welfare state and although it is not documented here this demand is not limited to financial benefits only but to such provisions as nurseries, better maternity care, abortion facilities, better public transport (which is more important to women and children who tend not to have access to private transport) and better housing provision, especially for single mothers.

The first extract presented here was written by Mary McIntosh in 1980 which discusses the development of contemporary feminist involvements in welfare.

SAQ This extract raises questions which you should be aware of:

1   Why is the family still so central to the feminist critique of the welfare state?

2   What demands are feminists now making of the state?

Feminism and social policy

During the 1970s, feminists developed a critique of the welfare system that was both sophisticated and damning. It began in a fragmentary way in the early seventies with specific protests about issues like the 'cohabitation rule' and the 'tax credit' proposals. There was a growing awareness that women figure prominently among the clients of social workers, the inmates of geriatric and psychiatric hospitals, the claimants of supplementary benefits — despite the fact that married and cohabiting women are not eligible for many benefits. There was resentment about the degrading way that women are treated when they need state benefits and state services . . .

This raised the whole question of women's dependence on men and the fact that women were second class citizens. The Women's Family Allowance Campaign against the Tory Government's 1972 tax-credit proposals focussed on the same problems. The family allowance, paid directly to a mother was preferable to the same, or even a greater, amount paid in tax credits through a father's pay packet. The model of the couple as a financial unit bore little relation to reality as many women experienced it. In the end, after we had defeated this aspect of the tax-credit scheme, the trade unions' reluctance to accept the loss of the child tax allowance that accompanied the improved child benefit only verified what we already knew: that money in a husband's pay packet was not equivalent to a direct payment to his wife.

In the context of the women's liberation movement, the developing awareness of women's relation to the welfare state was crystallised at the national conference in 1974. Elizabeth Wilson's pamphlet *Women and the Welfare State* (1974) was launched there and a new demand, for 'legal and financial independence', was adopted. The new demand, the fifth to be adopted by the movement, recognised clearly the relevance of the state in solving the problem of women's dependence upon men. The other demands (concerned with equal opportunities in jobs and training, equal pay, nurseries, abortion and contraception) all had a bearing on women's independence in their different ways. But this one, as the paper calling for it to be adopted expressed it, 'highlights the links between the state and the family, and the way in which the state systematically bolsters the dependent-woman family' (Gieve et al., 1974). It saw the relevance of state policy not merely to those categories of women who receive or are denied state benefits of various kinds — not merely to mothers and non-mothers, wives and non-wives, earners and non-earners — but to women as a whole category. For it saw how state policies play a part in constructing that category and in constructing the idea of the family in which it exists. All women *suffer from the stereotype of the woman as properly dependent upon a man. But all women also suffer in quite practical terms from the fact that there are few viable alternatives to such dependence.* (For an argument against this view, see Bennett et al., 1980.)

Since then, this critique of state policy has been detailed and sustained. Academic articles have been published (especially by Hilary Land, 1976, 1977), and so have pamphlets (for instance, Streather and Weir, 1974; Lister and Wilson, 1976). Many a parliamentary select committee and inter-departmental working party has been told of our views by various women's groups. Wider campaigns, like the rousing but in the end rather abortive one on wives' treatment under income tax, have been mounted. *What is disappointing is how little this critique has really affected thinking among other radicals about social policy.* Goodwill towards feminism expresses itself in manning the creche, going on the abortion demo and avoiding sexist styles of behaviour. But how many critics of the DHSS review of Supplementary Benefit a year or so ago — apart from women — argued against the aggregation of the income and resources of husband and wife? Yet separate treatment has been our demand ever since the first feminist critiques of the Beveridge Report in the early 1940s (see, for instance, Abbott and Bompas, 1943; Pierce, 1979) . . .

All of these critical approaches to social policy were the feminist version of the radical and marxist critiques of the 1960s and 1970s. The burden of these was that the welfare state is nothing of the kind: that it is not redistributive as between the social classes, but makes the working class pay for its own social casualties, that it does not even eliminate poverty at the bottom end of the scale, that it is not the harbinger of socialist provision according to need — neither in its style nor in its effects — and that it is an instrument of bourgeois control, forcing people to work and imposing standards of morality, decency and household management. To this, feminists add that the welfare state is especially oppressive to women, in that it harnesses them into the team that pulls the whole welfare charabanc along.

What was new, though, was that there was a clear recognition at the same time that women need state provision. Faced with a choice between a chancy dependence on a man on the one hand and dependence on the state or exploitation in waged work on the other, feminists opt for the state and the wage . . .

With all their problems, then, the state and the employer can be fought collectively and unlike modern marriage they are not intrinsically patriarchal. And whenever feminists have formulated the demand for the socialisation of housework and of personal care, it has been state provision rather than private commercial provision that they have had in mind.

I shall turn now to these more specific questions of feminist strategy. In some ways, the central problem is the same one that has plagued feminism ever since the achievement of the vote left the movement without a central rallying cry. The problem is whether to press for equality with men, usually in terms of legal, political and citizenship rights, or to press for greater support and respect for women in their roles as housewives and mothers: a right to an independent income and a recognition of the importance of their contribution . . .

Socialist feminists in the women's liberation movement have transcended the old divide in the sense that they have questioned not only masculinity and femininity, not only man's place and woman's place, but also the very existence of social division and difference based on sex. *We have firmly located the origin and support for this division in the family.* This does not mean that we locate it in individual kin-based households, but in the institution of the family, with its ideology, its imperatives and its constraints, which spread far beyond households themselves and both cause and enable the organisation of everything else to be marked by gender division. Women's liberation depends upon the radical transformation of that family. However, although there is much disagreement about the relation of that family system to capitalism, most socialist feminists agree on two things: that the specific character of women's oppression at present is related to the articulation between the family system and the wage system; and that we should start working now towards the transformation of the family system and that it will not automatically arrive along with socialism. Indeed, I would add that the family system is changing and is under great strain at present (and not only because of the resurgence of feminism), so that it is incumbent on us to play a part in determining what form that change takes.

On the whole we choose to campaign for those things that we know will both help the immediate problems of many women and also help to open up possibilities for further and more far-reaching change. The demand for 'disaggregation' in social security, income tax, student grants and so on, is a good example. The aggregation of the married couple into a tax unit and into a means-testable unit — however it may be dressed up in unisex clothing — represents women's dependence on their husbands. This is a dependence that is unreliable and degrading when it does exist and which in any case is a less common pattern than is often supposed, since most women are breadwinners, Hamill (1978). In terms of social security, disaggregation would mean that a married women who could not get a job could claim supplementary benefit regardless of her husband's income. But it would also mean that a married man would get a single person's benefit with no allowance for the wife; she would have to claim herself and fulfill the usual conditions: unless she was responsible for caring for small children or an invalid or something like that, she would have to sign on for employment.

This is a demand that comes out of our own experience. Several of the group which formulated it had suffered indignities and deprivation at the hands of the social security. Even so, the chief argument for it is not that thousands of women will be better off. It is that all women will have rights to full social security and that all men will lose the right to state back-up for keeping their wives in dependence. We realise that some women, especially older ones who have not had recent experience of going out to work, will be disadvantaged. We realise that forcing women onto the labour-market as it exists for them now is painful. But we believe that married women's dependence is in part responsible for their dreadful position in the labour-market, and the movement is simultaneously fighting for better pay and conditions at work, including the part-time and low-paid jobs that many women are forced to take . . .

The welfare system as it stands (or totters) is utterly dependent upon a specific construction of gender. The Department of Health and Social Security is well aware of that and it is time that critics of social policy were as well.

References

Elizabeth Abbot and Katherine Bompas, *The Woman Citizen and Social Security: A Criticism of the Proposals Made in the Beveridge Report as they affect Women*, London: Mrs. Bompas, 1941.

Sandra Allen, *et al.*, eds. *Conditions of Illusion*, Leeds: Feminist Books, 1974.

Michele Barrett and Mary McIntosh 'The Family Wage' *Capital and Class*, No. 11, 1980.

Fran Bennett, *et al.*, 'The Limitations of the Demand for Independence' *Politics and Power*, No. 1, 1980.

Anne Bottomley *et al.*, *The Cohabitation Handbook. A Woman's Guide to the Law*, Pluto Press, 1981.

Manuel Castella, 'Collective Consumption and Urban Contradictions in Advanced Capitalism' reprinted in Castells City. *Class and Power*, Macmillan, 1978.

Valerie Charlton, 'The Patter of Tiny Contradictions' *Red Rag*, No. 5, reprinted in Sandra Allen *et al.* eds, *op. cit.* 1974.

Equal Opportunities Commission, *Health and Safety Legislation: Should we Distinguish between Men and Women?* HMSO, 1979.

Carmel Flaskas and Betty Hounslow, 'Government Intervention and Right-Wing Attacks on Feminist Services' *Scarlet Woman* (Australia) No. 11, 1980.

Katherin Gieve, *et al.*, 'The Independence Demand' in Sandra Allen *et al.*, eds. 1974.

Patrice Grevet, *Besoins Populaires et Financement Public*, Paris, Editions Sociales, 1976.

Lynn Hamill, 'Wives as Sole and Joint Breadwinners', paper presented to the Social Science Research Council, Social Security Research Workshop, 1978.

Jane Humphries, 'Class Struggle and the persistence of the working-class family' *Cambridge Journal of Economics*, Vol. 1, No. 3, pp 241-58, 1977.

Jane Humphries, 'Protective Legislation, the Capitalist State and Working-Class Men: 1842 Mines Regulation Act' *Feminist Review*, No. 7, 1981.

B. L. Hutchins and A. Harrison, *A History of Factory Legislation*, 2nd edition, P. S. King and Son, London, 1911.

Hilary Land, 'Women: Supporters or Supported?' in Diana Barker and Sheila Allen, *Sexual Divisions and Society: Process and Change*, London: Tavistock, 1976.

Hilary Land, 'Social Security and the Division of Unpaid work in the Home and Paid Employment in the Labour Market' in Department of Health and Social Security, *Social Security Research Seminar*, London: HMSO, pp 43-61. 1977.

Hilary Land, 'The Family Wage' *Feminist Review*, No. 6, 1980.

Law Commission, *Family Law: The Financial Consequences of Divorce: The Basic Policy: A Discussion Paper.* (Law Com. No. 103) London, HMSO, Cmnd. 8041, 1980.

Jane Lewis, 'Eleanor Rathbone and the New Feminism During the 1920s' Unpublished mimeograph, 1973.

Ruth Lister and Leo Wilson, *The Unequal Breadwinner*, London: National Council for Civil Liberties, 1976.

Juliet Mitchell, *Psychoanalysis and Feminism,* London: Allen Lane, 1974.
Sylvie Pierce, 'Ideologies of Female Independence in the Welfare State:
Women's Response to the Beveridge Report' Paper given at British
Sociological Association Annual Conference, 1979.
Eleanor F. Rathbone, *Milestones: Presidential Addresses at the Annual Council
Meetings of NUSEC,* London, 1929.
Anne Bottomley *et al., The Cohabitation Handbook: A Woman's Guide to the
Law,* Pluto Press, 1981.
Jane Streather and Stuart Weir, *Social Insecurity: Single Mothers on Social
Security,* Child Poverty Action Group, Poverty Pamphlet No. 16, 1974.
Elizabeth Wilson, *Women and the Welfare State,* Red Rag Pamphlet No. 2,
1974.

This article is based on a paper given by the author at the Critical Social
Policy Conference, 'Crisis in the Welfare State' in November 1980.

(McIntosh, 1981, pp. 32-41).

For contemporary feminists, the central issue has been to struggle against
the state's reinforcement of an unequal sexual division of labour. But for
them, this does not mean retreating from state provided welfare, rather
they demand forms of welfare provision which will allow women to be
treated as independent. The family — and the ideology of the family — is
central to these struggles because the inequality of the sexual division of
labour is grounded in the family. It is the idea of women as wives and
mothers — as dependents — which informs and shapes current welfare
provision.

In her paper McIntosh refers to the Women's Family Allowance
Campaign of 1972 which was formed specifically to fight the Conservative
government's plan to abolish family allowances, which had been fought
for for so long by Eleanor Rathbone, and to replace them with tax credits
which would benefit the breadwinner rather than women and children.
This plan was defeated after sustained criticism from groups such as that
above and also the Child Poverty Action Group (CPAG), the Claimants'
Union and women in the Labour Party. It is nonetheless a useful example
of a particular feminist campaign on welfare provision and consequently
we have chosen an extract from a pamphlet produced by the Women's
Family Allowance Campaign. What is particularly interesting about this
campaign is the way in which it was transformed from an attempt to
preserve the status quo into demand to extend benefits to women. A
number of feminists went on to demand wages for housework. It
provides a good example of how a struggle over one issue led many
women to perceive the position of women in the family in a new way.

SAQ In reading the following extract consider how the state is perceived
by this campaigning group. But at the same time, consider why they
insist that a state income is so important for women outside waged work.

The Family Allowance Under Attack

What do we want?

The proposals *they* make for us limit us all over again. The demands *we*
make should be for things that would help us to break out of the roles and
structures that confine us. No one demand, or group of related demands, can
indicate all we want. But the Family Allowance Campaign has expressed our
desire for financial independence from men in a new way. We know how
important economic independence from men is if we are to live our own lives,
and if they are to have a chance to move without the burden of having to

support us. But in the past, demands for money for women have been expressed in a way that has simply led to more work for us. They have been in terms of getting a job outside the home, without seriously challenging the burden of work we do *in* the home — which has remained as our other, 'hidden' job. The Family Allowance Campaign has given practical expression to the idea of extending payment from the State for work women already do, work in the home.

We are beginning to get a sense of how crucial the work done in the home is to the economy, and how reluctant the State is to pay for this huge quantity of 'hidden' work. But just because it's not on their agenda, it doesn't mean that we shouldn't put it on ours. A demand for money for that work can do two things. It aims to bring us economic independence without bringing us more work. In doing so, it challenges the idea that 'home-making' is just a 'natural' expression of our femininity, a godgiven part of our relationship with children and men. It underlines the fact that housewives, in servicing men and rearing children in our society, are working for capital.

The threat to the Family Allowance, the threat to the little money that the State now pays to women, has highlighted how important that money is for women. The fact that such a small sum of money is so important gives us some idea of what a difference it would make if, instead of a pittance, we could make the State pay women a proper income.

(Fleming, 1973)   June 1973

"WELL, YOU SAID TO
PUT IT IN WRITING."

The state is identified as a body which currently reinforces women's dependency through its welfare system. But it offers the possibility of being different. It could be made to provide economic support for women in ways which would be free of the ties and dependency attaching to 'housekeeping money', or the pressure to take low paid work.

Not all feminists agreed that the logical extension of the demand to keep family allowances was the provision of an income for housewives. For many feminists the idea of the WLM was to free women from the drudgery of housework rather than to pay them to do it. Moreover many made the distinction between housework and childcare, and preferred to concentrate on transforming the conditions of childrearing rather than perpetuating the demand for full-time housewives. However, one point on which all feminists do agree is that the majority of welfare provision concerns women. This is a point made by Elizabeth Wilson in her article

'Feminism and Social Policy' in the Course Reader, and it is made in the next extract by the Claimants' Union in their 1982 pamphlet *Women and Social Security*. You will see that this document is polemical. It is not meant to provide an analysis so much as to drive home a simple point, namely that social security (and arguably social policy) is about women.

Social security is about women

Each week 14 million child benefit payments are paid to women. Each week 300,000 unsupported mothers claim supplementary benefit. Two-thirds of supplementary pensions paid to the retired go to women. By far the largest group dependant on social security payments is 'Women'.

Women are also the largest group of low paid employees in Britain. Despite Equal Pay legislation women's wages still lag well behind those of men. However women are not able to claim Family Income Supplement on top of their wages if there's a man around.

It is an interesting fact that the majority of D.H.S.S. employees are women. Furthermore, most of the ministers responsible for social security provision have been women. Judith Hart, Peggy Herbison, and Barbara Castle have all headed the social security machine.

Despite the enormous involvement of women in the social security system, it has *never* been run in our interests. The social security system reinforces the sexual division of labour in our society. Women are still treated mainly as child rearers and home minders. Women are denied benefits and discriminated against and constantly forced into financial dependence on men. It is men who are treated as 'breadwinners' and 'heads of households'. Women are seen merely as appendages of them — as mere 'dependants'.

Two aspects of income maintenance are changing under pressure from women: the national insurance system and the taxation system. But means tested supplementary benefits defies change at present. Supplementary benefit is based on 'the nuclear family/couple unit'. Here women are constantly humiliated by the refusal of means-testers to treat us as individuals, and to pay us income in our own right. We are intimidated by 'liable relative officers', spied on by 'special investigators' and subjected to denials under the 'cohabitation rule'.

But women are refusing to be treated as second class citizens any longer. We are fighting back. We hope this pamphlet will help you fight with us.

(Claimants' Union, 1982)

In the extract from Mary McIntosh's paper she argues for the importance of feminists joining (and hopefully transforming) traditional Left groups and organizations and being prepared to engage at all levels in putting forward feminist analyses and proposals. This has not been easy for modern feminists who have rejected the *form* and *content* of traditional politics and who feel that the essence of the new feminism can be threatened by absorption into mainstream politics. At the same time it is realised that in order to be influential it is often necessary to have the support of established and powerful groups (for example the National Abortion Campaign's alliance with the TUC to resist reactionary reforms to the abortion law.)

One example of the influence of feminism on established forms of political activity is the feminist presence in the Child Poverty Action Group (CPAG) and in the National Council for Civil Liberties (NCCL). Like the early feminists who were concerned with the plight of poor women, their feminist grand-daughters are again struggling to reveal how poverty is a condition which primarily affects women — especially those with children. Consequently (like Anna Martin and Eleanor Rathbone) they concentrate a great deal on child benefits and maternity benefits. Unlike the early feminists though, they combine this with an attack on the rigid structure of the family that the state imposes through its system of welfare provision. The pamphlet *The Family in the Firing Line* produced jointly by the CPAG and the NCCL is an example of this. This pamphlet documents in detail the sort of welfare provision available to women in 1981. It concentrates on discrimination on the one hand and inadequate provision on the other. Because of the nature of the pamphlet which is intended to expose the inadequacy of government (both Conservative and Labour policy), it does not adopt an explicit political position or espouse a particular form of feminist analysis. Nonetheless it is possible to read 'between the lines' so to speak to identify the authors' views on state intervention in the family and the consequences of particular state policies.

SAQ Why do you think the authors concentrate on maternity rights and the consequences of state policy in this area? Besides improving these rights, what other major suggestion do they make for reforming the welfare system?

Sex discrimination in social security: In addition to cuts in benefits which hurt families with children, the social security system itself imposes a specific pattern of family life through a set of sex-discriminatory rules, which mean that families who want to, or have to, live differently from that pattern are penalised financially. The best that both this and the previous Government have seen fit to do, however, is to give way to a legally-binding Common Market Directive which in 1983 will *begin* to free *parts* of our social security system from discrimination against women. Only in 1983 will some married and cohabiting women have the opportunity to claim FIS and SB. And not until 1984 will they be able to claim the extra additions to national insurance benefits in respect of their dependent children on the same terms as men. The Directive will still leave some areas of sex discrimination free to continue . . .

Clearly, even when the Directive is implemented, a number of fundamental questions will still need to be resolved if women's financial dependence on men is not to be an inherent feature of our social security system. In particular, thought needs to be given to the question of how to move away from a system which is based on the 'aggregation' of resources and needs of a couple to one which treats husband and wife as individuals in their own right for the purposes of social security benefits — and taxation also.

Maternity rights

In the context of the longstanding debate about whether mothers should take paid jobs or stay at home with their children, it is sobering to note that if married women did not go out to work, the number of families living in poverty would increase *four-fold*, according to estimates published by the Central Policy Review Staff.

The Government, instead of improving maternity rights and child benefit, expanding women's employment opportunities and providing the day care required to give women a really genuine choice in the 'go to work/stay at home' decision, are, it seems, only too happy to see married women pushed out of the labour market, because it makes the unemployment figures look less alarming. The revival of the 'mothers-should-be-at-home-for-their-children's-own-good' line is the ideology that inevitably accompanies the economics in which unemployment rockets and public expenditure plummets. The upshot is that the ordinary working woman sees her terms and conditions at work threatened and the value of her maternity and child benefits undermined.

Maternity pay: The 1980 Employment Act, while leaving intact the right to six weeks' maternity pay and 29 weeks' leave after the birth of a baby, introduces various new administrative procedures which make it more difficult in practice for a woman to exercise her right to return to her job. Indeed, for women working in firms which employ fewer than six people, the right to return has been completely abolished. And in firms of *all* sizes, the employer now has much more scope to prevent a woman coming back to the same job she held before her maternity leave. Even before the restrictions introduced under the Employment Act, it was found that considerable numbers of women employed in small firms were not getting the rights to which they were entitled by law. The Government did, however, bow to pressure from various organisations concerned with risks to mothers' and babies' health and make one welcome change in employment law relating to maternity. All women are now to have the right to time off work with no loss of pay for their ante-natal care.

Maternity grant: Another welcome change has been the announcement that as from 1982 the £25 lump-sum maternity grant will be made non-contributory; in other words, all mothers will receive it, regardless of their work record. But why wait until 1982? It will cost nothing to introduce, because making it non-contributory reduces the administrative costs. Yet there are 60,000 mothers a year who do not qualify for the grant and they are usually those most at risk because of their youth and/or poverty. Mothers on supplementary benefit now have a right to single payments for maternity needs, but the right has not been well-publicised and problems still remain in getting adequate grants from the DHSS.

The sum of £25 has remained unchanged since 1969 and, according to a parliamentary answer to Jo Richardson MP, it should have been £99.50 by November 1980 if its value had been maintained. The *actual* value of £25 today, compared to 1969, is just £6.29.

Maternity allowance: The weekly maternity allowance (at present £20.65) has just been cut in real terms. Married women, of course, cannot top up their allowance with supplementary benefit (because no woman who is married or thought to be cohabiting can claim SB). They will also suffer a particularly harsh injustice when the earnings-related supplement is phased out and finally abolished, unless the Employment Protection (Consolidation) Act is amended. The change needed is to give women six weeks' maternity pay on *full* pay, rather than 90 per cent only, as is the case at present. The reason for making it 90 per cent in the first place was the assumption that most women would get an earnings-related supplement which would bring their total weekly income back up to its normal level. Many women, of course, do not qualify for a supplement at all, partly because their earnings have been too low and partly because the relevant tax year for calculating the supplement often coincides with a period a couple of years or so previously when the woman was at home caring for another child and therefore had no earnings. The abolition of the earnings-related supplement would only become acceptable in the context of a higher basic national insurance benefit plus better statutory employer's maternity pay. (The latter, of course, is totally refundable to employers from the state's Maternity Pay Fund which itself has a surplus large enough to help find more generous maternity payments.) . . .

We are the only EEC country, for example, that imposes a service qualification on working women before they are entitled to maternity rights from their employer. In cash benefits, our £25 maternity grant is negligible compared to the grant of over £300 a Belgian mother receives for her first child, or the £460 received by a French woman in combined pre-natal and post-natal grants. Comparisons with non-EEC Sweden are even more diminishing for Britain: under the Swedish 'parental insurance' scheme, parents can take up to 10 months' paid leave after the birth of a child and can divide the period between them if and how they wish. Such European comparisons have to be used with care (for example, medical services have to be paid for in some countries). Nevertheless, they do suggest that Britain compares very badly with many other countries.

The only attempt the Government has made to review maternity pay and benefits was conducted on a 'no-cost' basis; it attracted no support and, thankfully, has been abandoned.

(Coussins and Coote, 1981)

The focus on maternity rights in part reflects the tradition of feminist concern with motherhood as women's most economically vulnerable situation. But it is also a focus because of the contemporary political context in which those rights are being eroded together with an ideology which emphasizes the virtues of women staying at home. The other major issue they deal with is the removal of the earnings-related supplement from National Insurance benefits. They argue this should not have been removed without a substantial increase in the basic level of benefits.

The main argument of the feminist in the 1970s and early 1980s has not been to dismantle the welfare state and to reject state provision but to point out how the current system reproduces women's dependency on men and consequently reinforces their disadvantageous position outside the family in waged work.

2.2 CONCLUSION

The primary goal of feminists in the field of social policy has been not only to challenge forms of sexual discrimination (e.g. the way in which Family Income Supplement is available to married men but not married women) but to challenge the very premiss on which the whole structure of welfare benefits is based — namely the reliance on the family unit and its implied dependency of the wife as a basis for the distribution of benefits. This is not an isolated campaign, it is part of the whole ethos of the WLM and is linked to other struggles through its analysis of patriarchal relations in which the family is a primary feature. Unlike earlier feminist campaigns, particularly those in the 1940s and 1950s, modern feminists are not content with the concept of equal-but-different. Indeed the liberal concept of equality is itself under scrutiny with the realization that equal provision does little to alter underlying structural inequalities between men and women. Contemporary feminists therefore are not just looking for equal provision in state benefits but a welfare state which recognises women's structurally unequal position and which works to overcome this.

3 FABIANISM

Since the early 1970s the apparent post-war social democratic consensus has begun to break up in the face of deepening economic recession in Britain. The expansion of welfare had always assumed a basis of managed economic growth, and this could no longer be guaranteed. The alternative financing of welfare — through redistribution from the relatively well paid (though not necessarily wealthy) to the poor has been a focus of political hostility. The rising acceptability of 'free-market' political ideology — with its identification of welfare as a burden on the taxpayer — has been the most visible signal of this change. But these economic and political changes have also had their impact on Fabianism.

It seems that Fabianism has fractured. While it is true that the classification of Fabians was always arbitrary to some extent and always contained divergent views, in the current situation it is difficult to establish where the intellectual and political centre of Fabianism may be found. In this section, then, we indicate some of the directions in which Fabians (or perhaps, ex-Fabians) have moved in recent years.

These different movements reflect a number of major issues in the contemporary politics of welfare. For the Fabians, the growing weight of evidence about the failure of the welfare state to achieve redistribution or solve poverty is a matter of central concern, leading to very divergent ideas of the possible responses to these failures. Alongside this, Fabianism and its conception of welfare have been at the heart of the attack from the 'free market' ideology of welfare. Fabianism was inextricably linked to the expansion of welfare through the state, and through the role of 'expertise' in planning and executing welfare policy. These two themes have been identified in the revival of laissez-faire thought as inefficient state monopolies, and the excessive power of bureaucrats and professionals, respectively.

Our first extract is taken from an article by Adrian Webb which appeared in a Fabian collection called *Labour and Inequality.* In this article, Webb assessed the record of the 1974-9 Labour government in the personal social services. Our extract focuses on Webb's discussion of the policy implications of the desire for equality. He deals with the dilemmas of trying to relate this goal to the practice of state welfare in the personal social services.

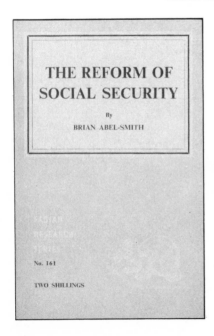

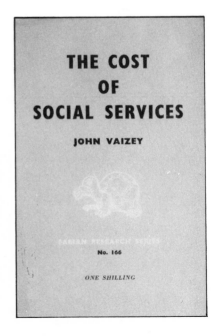

SAQ What do you think is Webb's primary concern in this analysis?

The Personal Social Services

An absence of concern for equality?

The post-war debate on equality and redistribution has virtually by-passed the personal social services. Unlike such services as education, housing or even health, relatively few attempts have been made systematically to gather data which would answer such questions as: who benefits; or, do these services reinforce or modify wider patterns of inequality? This neglect reflects the generally low status accorded to these services; even now their 'take' of public expenditure, compared with that of the more established social services, is insufficient to exert much impact on national inequality.

There is a widespread assumption that the 'benefits' of the personal social services do find their way to the poor and the working classes. Any intention there may have been at the time of the Seebohm report of producing a universal service to set alongside the NHS has been destroyed by the twin forces of rising demand and public expenditure restraint which characterised the second half of the 1970s. Despite a few faltering steps towards a universal service, the personal social services have not fully escaped from the residual model of their Poor Law origins. The constant concern is to identify the most needy as a basis for allocating scarce resources, rather than to offset the 'overly successful' use of services by the middle classes. There are middle class clients, there are real issues of inequality and there is real interest in the pursuit of equality, but the very failure to establish a comprehensive service in the universal mould means that one of the major preoccupations in other services the distribution of services between classes or income groups is less fiercely debated.

What are the personal social services?

For the purposes of this chapter, the personal social services are taken to comprise the work of local authority social services departments and of voluntary and informal care and provision for similar client groups. This approach excludes the probation and after-care service, but it includes a great mass of imprecisely defined non-statutory work. One must also recognise the importance of privately purchased or produced services, ranging from elderly and disabled people who buy domestic help on the 'open market' to socially dependent people who live in hotels, private boarding houses or 'homes', rather than in a private household.

The Fabian Society: developing welfare expertise

The personal social services can only be understood and analysed if they are conceived as part of a 'mixed economy of welfare'. The balances and shifts between the various components of this 'mixed economy' must be counted as a central issue in any discussion of equality. In 'real' manpower terms, at least, the 'professional' statutory services are overshadowed by the volunteer sector. The informal care provided by kin, neighbours and friends is extensive and diverse, although not easily quantified. Changes in the statutory sector must therefore be expected to ripple throughout a much wider 'system' and vice versa . . .

Equality: the outstanding dilemmas

A concern for equality has characterised the personal social services throughout the past decade or so, despite the lack of quantitative studies of redistribution. The impact has been on the ideologies and nascent theories which underpin practice rather than on specific or general objectives. An increase in resources could remove some of the disappointments. Both residential and community care services could be extended, improved in quality, and made more flexible. The status of 'simple' care could be enhanced by focusing more attention on the role of domiciliary, day and informal care. An enhanced share of training opportunities for care staff would be a key to such improvements. Similarly, greater imagination and collaboration, backed by extra resources, could bring more advisory, supportive and socially and culturally enriching care to the handicapped, the mentally ill and to the elderly. Resources are a necessary means of moving away from the 'emergency service' syndrome which afflicts this most neglected of the social services.

A second issue, that of charges and means tests, raises a problem which has not been made explicit, that of equity between consumers and potential consumers. If charges are a source of stigma and non-uptake of service, they offend against one of our concepts of equality; if they enable service to be extended, they may promote equality. The personal social services include a variety of different contexts in which charges are, or can be, applied. Charges for residential care for the elderly primarily represent a substantial transfer of resources from the social security system to local authorities and are comparatively non-controversial. Those imposed on the parents of children in local authority residential care are potentially far more controversial and may represent a source of additional stigma for families who are reluctant users of child care services. Charges on domiciliary services occupy a middle ground: they are controversial but they do not contain 'punitive' overtones. Charging policies differ enormously and there is unfortunately little factual evidence, as opposed to assumptions and assertion, on which to base policy. Even the economic viability of charging for some services (such as home helps) is unclear. At present, the question of charges poses an apparent and unresolved choice between the equality to be achieved through a possibly more extensive, but means tested, service and that achieved through a universal, free, but admittedly under-financed, service.

A third problem — that of territorial inequalities — is by no means simple or receding. The national concern for inner city areas reflected in the rate support grant formula may be an appropriate redistributive strategy, but not all shire counties have the resource base from which to provide good services in rural areas and by no means all of those which have, do so. Rural deprivation has been greatly neglected and it bears heavily on the personal social services in many county districts. The physical isolation induced by declining rural transport services exacerbates the problems of the elderly and disabled in particular and adds to the cost of maintaining services. Since local government reorganisation in 1974, most shire counties have been faced with inequalities of service between the old county and the old county borough areas and territorial justice has been a key policy issue for some of the new social services departments.

A fourth example of complexity centres on the growing enthusiasm for informal and voluntary care. At worst it is unreflective jingoism, but this worst manifestation was a predictable reaction to 'resource shock'. The potential, and the limits, of alternatives to state services are beginning to attract more serious attention. Whether the right questions are yet being asked in a coherent way — from the equality, or other, perspectives — is another matter. The danger presently remains that these alternatives could be developed and used with too high an expectation of saving money in the state sector. To paraphrase Richard Titmuss's famous dictum on selectivity, we most urgently need to establish that infrastructure of universal, publicly financed provision which will enable the non-statutory alternatives to grow in appropriate ways. This is profoundly a matter of philosophy and objectives and not merely of giving a bit more public money to voluntary agencies or beseeching families and neighbours to do more for the socially dependent.

One final problem for the future arises from the tendency of an inadequately financed policy of community care to transfer the burden of care to the families, neighbours and friends of the people in need of care or to volunteers. Surprisingly, there has been little attempt to document the extent and consequences of this phenomenon.

Nevertheless, there is a sense of failure and disillusionment among many personal social services staff — admittedly counter-balanced by optimism and sheer determination — which is too fundamental to be explained wholly by the shortage of resources. It is intimately connected with the concern for equality.

Even at the level of general philosophy, some problems were already apparent from the beginning of the seventies. A structural view of causal processes and policy solutions is highly likely to lead to frustration: structural change depends essentially on the effectiveness of social and economic policies outside the control of the personal social services. The paradox of commitment and impotence surfaced in the Community Development Projects, and more indirectly in corporate planning and the growth of community work within social services departments. Impotence in the face of frustrated hopes has been a large part of the experience of personal social services staffs throughout the seventies.

This experience has raised a fundamental question of legitimacy. The structural view of causality was sufficiently widely accepted for the wider failure to fund egalitarian policies to undermine the legitimacy of much social service work from within. The experience of failure to achieve the more ambitious hopes of more optimistic days has been generalised. The attempt merely to ameliorate inequalities — material and social — tends to be derided or undervalued. But amelioration, in context, is a legitimate and necessary function of the personal social services.

Similarly, by reference merely to the raised expectations of visible outcomes instead of the underlying causes and increased social stress, public and political reactions have signalled a lack of confidence in these services from without. The problem which these reactions highlight is partly one of morale, but also one of theory and philosophy and of a lack of widely shared understandings. The personal social services are beginning to reverberate to the question: what are we achieving with the use of even those scarce resources we possess? Part of the response must be the evolution of a more sophisticated analysis of the different types of egalitarian objectives which can appropriately be pursued through the personal social services.

(Webb, 1980, pp. 279-80, 286-95)

Webb's review of government policy seems to be directed not merely at identifying the limitations on resources, but at the political and professional failures to identify and clarify the goal of egalitarianism for personal social services policy. For him, this failure has made both the rational formulation and assessment of policies very difficult. Part of the task he identifies is the 'evolution of a more sophisticated analysis' of egalitarian goals. This concern to develop more rational and systematic formulation and assessment remains true to one of the central themes of Fabianism: the key role which is given to 'expertise' in planning.

Our second extract — from Peter Townsend — puts forward a more radical set of proposals. In the best Fabian tradition, these proposals come out of a massive piece of detailed research into poverty, but the proposals themselves do not seem to be directed at better informing the policy-making process. In Townsend's hands, poverty moves from being an issue of rational discussion to find the 'best solution', to a recognition of real social conflicts over available resources.

Townsend may be developing his arguments on the basis of Beveridge, but the movement away from this starting point is very clear. He is far more concerned with explicit issues of redistribution. He strengthens the demand for the right to work, and talks emphatically about the need for any new system to be democratized. Here the boundary between Fabian and Socialist analyses is perhaps more blurred than ever before.

SAQ Why does Townsend argue that we need to move from the idea of a national minimum to a more redistributive solution to poverty?

The elimination of poverty

[Three principle models of social policy may be advanced]: (a) conditional welfare for the few; (b) minimum rights for the many; and (c) distributional justice for all. In the course of the twentieth century, social policy has been dominated by one or other of the first two principles or by a mixture of both principles. One of the purposes of this book has been to call attention to at least the possibility of applying the third principle extensively in constructing policy. In the late 1960s and early 1970s, despite protestations to the contrary, successive governments invoked the first principle with renewed vigour . . .

The second principle is more persuasive, but falls far short of the expectations of its advocates. The assumption is not only that the hierarchical social and economic system requires generous underpinning rather than recasting, but that it *can* be so underpinned. History throws doubt on this assumption. Basic needs have tended to be defined in historical, absolute terms instead of contemporaneous, relative or social terms — and even such needs have not been met in practice. For example, Beveridge adopted the meagre definition of necessities outlined by Rowntree at a 'subsistence' basis for national insurance benefits. He intended these benefits to be at a level sufficient to guarantee subsistence without resort to means-tested supplementation. This was the cardinal principle, as he himself proclaimed it, of his plan. In over thirty years since the national insurance scheme was enacted, this principle has never been fulfilled. Governments have shrunk from fulfilling it; perhaps because of the implications for public expenditure, but more likely because of the threat that would be posed to the lower reaches of the wage system, and more generally to the kind of employment system appropriate to a capitalist or even 'mixed' economy. The 1834 Poor Law Commission's principle of less eligibility lives on in the definition of levels and conditions of social security benefits.

I am suggesting that there is an in-built tension, and even contradiction, in the application of the principle of a national minimum to a market economy. A minimum is hard to establish alongside or underneath a wage-earning and property-owning hierarchy — except at a very low level. It becomes hard to maintain when the number of dependants at each end of the age-scale increases and, as a result of the economy meeting fluctuating fortunes, more people of so-called active age are made redundant or unemployed. Either wages and transfer payments alike have to be brought under the control of a statutory incomes policy, or the payment of money for goods and services has to give way to the provision of free goods and services.

The third principle of distributional justice for all reflects a more adequate theory of poverty and a better prescription of the policies required to defeat it ... There is ... maldistribution of types as well as amounts of resources. There are large numbers in poverty or on its margins, a constant movement into and out of poverty, and there are close relationships between low income or denial of access to income and *systems* or *structure* of resources. Enlargement of access is as important as greater equality of distribution. Thus, the rights of both disabled and non-disabled people, including the elderly, to obtain gainful employment can and must be extended — by legal and social means ...

Wealth, including land, property and other assets, can and must be distributed more widely as well as more evenly. This can be done by the enlargement of the direct rights of the individual as well as by extending public ownership. Rights to housing, for example, should be more widely shared in the sense that the disparity between owner-occupation and tenancy should be reduced by common definition of the rights to succession and adaptation as well as to space and amenities.

Another example is incomes policy. The separation of the payment of earnings from that of social security and the lack of access of married women to cash incomes of their own would be reviewed. Income might be paid from a common, public, source or by a small number of agencies regulated by common principles. An incomes policy would be negotiated annually for workers and non-workers alike. It would therefore absorb the social security scheme, though there would continue to be direct payments as there are at present, for example, to disabled and elderly people, and child allowances drawn at the Post Office by mothers. New cash allowances would be payable to many categories of married women, by virtue of their work. With more adequate provisions in cash for many people currently labelled 'dependants' of the wage-earner or family, there could be fewer grades of payment to the 'employed' and 'self-employed' within a much smaller ratio between top and bottom of the income scale. Or perhaps the state could regulate a policy for a basic income for the entire population, leaving provision for some topping up by local or industrial negotiation. The further implication is that, given social regulation of incomes and of the distribution of other resources, the tax system would be substantially reduced as an intermediary in the allocation and reallocation of resources ...

A transformation of work organization and social relations would be required to legitimate such changes and secure public approval for them. The hierarchy of earnings depends on an elaborate division of labour and the supervision of each grade by the personnel in an ascendant grade. The hierarchy of social class depends in substantial part on the unequal distribution of wealth, including land, housing and other property. By reorganizing production in smaller collaborative units or teams, interchanging workers or arranging spells of manual and non-manual work and dividing possessions and property more evenly, the possibilities might at least be indicated.

An effective assault on poverty would therefore include:

1. *Abolition of excessive wealth.* The wealth of the rich must be substantially reduced by different policies and a statutory definition of maximum permissible wealth in relation to the mean agreed.

2.   *Abolition of excessive income.* Top salaries or wages must be substantially reduced in relation to the mean and a statutory definition of maximum permissible earnings (and income) agreed.

3.   *Introduction of an equitable income structure and some breaking down of the distinction between earners and dependants.* At the logical extreme this might involve the withdrawal of personal income taxation and of the social security benefits scheme, and the payment of tax-free incomes according to a publicly agreed and controlled schedule by occupational category and skill, but also by need or dependency — which would cover a relatively narrow span of variability; together with a substantial increase in corporation or payroll taxes. A less radical and therefore less effective solution would be the adoption of a more comprehensive income policy than the policies primarily of wage restraint which have operated since the early 1960s, together with a more coordinated social security benefit scheme with higher relative levels of benefit.

4.   *Abolition of unemployment.* For all over the age of compulsory education a legally enforceable right to work is needed, with a corresponding obligation on the part of employers, the government and especially local authorities, to provide alternative types of employment. This right would apply at different, including severe, levels of disablement, and would apply also to the elderly.

5.   *Reorganization of employment and professional practice.* There must be further innovations in public ownership, industrial democracy and collaborative instead of hierarchical work structures; restraint on the growth of power under the guise of professional and managerial autonomy, and encouragement of self-dependence and a high level of universal education.

6.   *Reorganization of community service.* There must be a corresponding growth of rights and hence responsibilities for members of local communities, with abolition of the distinction between owner-occupiers and tenants, and social-service support for the individual and family at home rather than in institutions.

It would be wrong to suggest that any of this is easy or even likely. The citadels of wealth and privilege are deeply entrenched and have shown tenacious capacity to withstand assaults, notwithstanding the gentleness of their legal, as distinct from the ferocity of their verbal, form. Yet we have observed the elaborate hierarchy of wealth and esteem, of which poverty is an integral part. If any conclusion deserves to be picked out from this report as its central message it is this, with which, some time, the British people must come to terms . . .

(Townsend, 1979, pp. 922-26)

Townsend argues that the concept of a national minimum is fundamentally ill-conceived because it can never satisfactorily deal with those groups on the margins of the defined minimum level. The idea of a minimum does not recognise the way in which poverty is structurally located in the whole pattern of wealth, income and resource distribution.

One of the elements in the break-up of Fabianism has been the fracturing of party politics. This is most sharply visible in the movement of some Labour politicians (Shirley Williams, David Owen, etc.) to form the Social Democratic Party. You may remember reading an extract from Shirley Williams in Unit 1, which discussed the need to decentralize welfare and make it more participatory. This concern to increase the involvement of voluntary agencies and to emphasize 'community care' is parallelled by many academic and professional voices, and seems to offer a movement away from the old 'collectivism' and expertise of the Fabians.

Our final extract here is taken from David Owen. In it he discusses inequality and how social democracy should respond to it. When reading it you should note how his proposals retain something of the Fabian 'technical' and managerial approach to social problems.

SAQ What relationship does Owen see between the proposals for responding to inequality, and the social democratic commitments to decentralization?

Overall the income maintenance system is now regarded with a good deal of cynicism by claimants, administrators and by the general public. A costly bureaucracy has been created to disburse large sums of public money and it cannot even be argued that any substantial reduction of poverty has resulted. A variety of reforms to the system can be suggested, ranging from the uprating of benefits to proposals designed to integrate the tax and welfare systems. A minimal strategy, merely to improve the existing system, would be to alter the workings of means-tests in order to increase the rate of take-up of benefits and to reduce the unpleasant tensions felt by claimants and social security officers. The amount of administrative discretion over supplementary benefit could be reduced, greater publicity could be given to the availability of benefits, and combined assessment schemes for benefits could be used to reduce administrative costs. There is some scope for changes of this nature but at best such changes are unlikely either to reduce costs substantially or to remove the stigma attached to the claiming of means-tested benefits. In addition, changes of this nature are also likely to produce further complications such as the intensification of the poverty trap or an increase in the length of forms. In recent years the take-up of supplementary benefit and family income supplement has greatly improved and the problem of disincentives is now greater than that of take-up.

Other, more far-reaching, policy options are, however, open — although it should be admitted that they are likely to involve either increased costs for higher benefits or considerable administrative changes for the Inland Revenue and the Department of Health and Social Security. Changes of a more radical nature cannot take place rapidly or even within the lifetime of one parliament and will require a degree of cross-party consensus, such as was achieved over the original Beveridge proposals, on a long-term strategy to help the poor. This consensus will be difficult to achieve but if we are to take seriously the needs of the poorest of our society the political parties must recognise the need to compromise and, as was done successfully in 1975 over the new state pensions legislation, plan together for the future. Achieving a synthesis of views in social policy is a constructive task for Parliamentary Select Committees.

The major options which are feasible are threefold: we can either drastically increase the levels of basic benefits, or replace the present social security and taxation systems by a reverse income tax, or move to a system of tax credits. The first strategy would aim to raise social insurance benefits to provide a guaranteed minimum income and to extend insurance to groups which at present rely on supplementary benefit. Further, a small degree of co-ordination of taxation and social security could also be achieved by raising the tax threshold to at least the supplementary benefit level. These changes could be undertaken entirely within the existing government institutions and would reduce the costs of administration by lifting groups of claimants off means-tested benefits. Take-up of benefits would also be increased by a reduction in means-testing and the poverty trap would be eased by a reduced dependence on Family Income Supplement. However, this strategy would involve a reform of the contribution conditions of the social insurance system and would necessitate a large increase in spending on universal benefits. Reform of the contributory nature of national insurance is long overdue and a number of feasible options exist for its replacement by a social security tax — but the main objection to the raising of universal benefits is that this is likely to be very costly, even after taking into account possible savings through the reduction of means-testing. These increased costs could be financed by the reduction or removal of tax relief for married couples or on mortgage interest payments. The strategy remains perfectly feasible and could be achieved given the political will; but it is possible that administrative reforms such as the introduction of a Reverse Income Tax, might be equally viable and less costly.

A tax credit scheme which was once seen as solving many problems is now less popular. It would replace personal tax allowances and family allowances by tax credits and any excess tax credit over tax due would be paid to the claimant. All national insurance benefits would become taxable, with everyone having to file a tax return, although those receiving only supplementary benefit would still be catered for by a separate system. Tax credits would increase the workload of the Inland Revenue and it is unlikely that this would be offset by administrative savings in the provision of supplementary benefits since many benefits would still need to be provided. Depending on the level at which the poverty line is fixed some supplementary benefit claimants would be raised above supplementary benefit levels, and the problem of take-up would be solved since payments would be automatic and the system would be simpler both to administer and to understand. Many of the existing means-tests would remain and with them a poverty trap — since supplementary benefit would be retained for many one-parent families and many of the unemployed. Like the strategy relying on increased rates of benefits, the tax credits scheme is difficult to cost, but a tentative estimate, for 1978, was that an increase in social security payments of £5,000 million was not unrealistic.

Reverse income tax would pay benefits, equivalent to seven-tenths of the deficit, to individuals whose incomes fell below a poverty line. Unemployment benefit, supplementary benefit, retirement pensions and sickness benefits would be replaced, along with employees' national insurance contributions Entitlement to reverse taxes would be calculated at the end of the financial year, with those in urgent need being able to receive cash by instalment payment. The reverse income tax would involve the Inland Revenue processing a tax return for every tax unit in the country and to a certain extent it would be responsible for the extra function of administering means-tests for families requiring immediate assistance. Alternatively, this function could remain with a much smaller Supplementary Benefits Commission. With reverse income tax a poverty trap would remain high because of high marginal tax rates, although marginal tax rates could be tapered to minimise the poverty trap. The income tax system would also lose much of its capacity as a tool of macro-economic management if short term changes in Pay As You Earn are ruled out as likely to impose hardship on the poor. The extent of the poverty trap which would remain would depend on the level of benefits set and benefit levels would have to be very carefully constructed to maintain incentives. Tax changes, for the purpose of economic management, could be balanced by changes in the level of benefits for the poor or by differential tax rates for different categories of taxpayer. Computerisation of the PAYE system offers the possibility of fully implementing a reverse income tax by 1986/87 since the increase in the number of tax-paying units required by a reverse income tax will be able to be dealt with more economically by computer than by the present manual system . . .

The only way of achieving a more equitable distribution of income in a democracy is to secure a greater awareness by the mass of the population of the facts about poverty, and by greater diffusion of wealth-holding. The cost for the social security system of an effective anti-poverty strategy will be very great and the taxes necessary to provide for such social security will be very high. Unless more people can feel secure and satisfied by their present and future standard of living they will resist paying such tax levels. Additional incomes from a share in profits and the security afforded by an ownership of assets is still the prerogative of the few. What is needed is to widen the definition of standard of living from a comparison of income to a concept that embraces asset-holding, whether in terms of home ownership, secure rented accommodation, shares or savings, and security, with the ability to benefit fully in our society from access to a good education service and health service — and to have confidence in the financial and care provision available in old age, sickness or disablement. It is this wider concept of the social wage, where the taxpayer sees his or her standard of living in broader terms than the after tax figure on the wage slip, that will cause the voter's resistance to paying tax to alleviate the poverty of others to be moderated. For the democratic, decentralising socialist, nationalisation is neither a necessary nor a sufficient condition for social change of this kind: reliance must be placed on changing people's attitudes, on promoting industrial democracy, and on industrial co-operatives, wider share ownership and, above all, wider home ownership.

(Owen, 1981, pp. 90-99)

Owen's proposals seem to contain a very varied approach to the issue of inequality. It is possible to identify some Fabian traces: the publicizing of the 'facts' about poverty, the rational discussion of solutions, and the creation of 'cross-party consensus'. The possible solutions themselves are cast in a traditionally Fabian way: assessing the administrative and technical issues of their implementation. To this is added a rather different statement about expanding rights, security and industrial democracy. The divergences within Fabianism are very accurately captured by the distance between Owen and Townsend in their approaches to inequality.

3.1 CONCLUSION

This emerging diversity of Fabianism represents the response to the collapse of the post-war welfare consensus in which Fabianism played a dominant role. In the three extracts we have considered it is possible to identify elements and continuities of the Fabian tradition, but perhaps only Webb represents a direct continuation. In a sense, both Townsend and Owen — in their very different ways — have taken elements of Fabianism into new directions.

An assessment of contemporary Fabianism, then, must accept that not all the traditional elements are held in common. The basing of policy on detailed knowledge and the 'facts' of inequality and poverty remains a central issue. Both Webb and Owen appear to hold the conception of a rational assessment of policy goals and means within the state. By contrast Townsend's broader strategy reflects on the resistance of the 'citadels of wealth and privilege' to change.

The family remains a central unit for Fabian analysis and policy elaboration, perhaps indicating the lack of effect achieved by feminist criticisms of orthodox social policy. Differences however are visible in approaches to questions of expertise and professionalism. Webb addresses the questions of policy formulation within the traditional framework of rational administration, while Owen mixes an administrative discussion of benefit and tax systems with a plea for greater democratization. Townsend, by contrast, makes strategic proposals which fall outside the orthodox structure of welfare policy and administration, by insisting that policies about poverty cannot be conceived apart from the overall structure of British society. It remains an open question which of these divergent movements will ultimately come to be identified as British Fabianism in the 1980s.

4 SOCIALISM AND WELFARE

The shift of Fabianism from its 'rightful place' at the centre of debates about the welfare state has had a remarkable effect on debates within the more explicitly socialist tradition. In the first place, it has allowed for some fundamental criticisms of the 'welfare state' which would not have been made — or at any rate not been given much attention — until the last decade or so. Thus in the first extract from Friend and Metcalf an attempt is made to explore some of the contradictions of Beveridge's legacy — in particular the way in which concessions on welfare can be turned into means of controlling rather than (or — most charitably — as well as) helping the poor. They challenge the traditional emphasis on the family, arguing that it has been a means of control rather than assistance.

The Friend and Metcalf critique is clearly within the tradition which heartily distrusts the state as ultimately being the product more of pressures from capital and big business than pressures from below, and they begin to suggest that it is important for the local working class to define its own needs, rather than, as they argue, being managed from above. This theme runs through recent socialist literature although socialists writing in this field seem to take a rather more optimistic view of the ways in which the state may be used or transformed.

Paradoxically, perhaps, as some doubts about the state's role are expressed by the Fabians, more explicitly socialist authors are embracing it more firmly and in the process attempting to shape it rather differently. Meacher's paper (the second extract) is closest to the traditional Labour Fabian approach in so far as the state is viewed as an instrument which can be redirected in positive ways. Walker (third extract) sees the state as a less homogeneous entity arising instead out of and being reconstituted by pressures from different classes and social groups (including professionals). But in practice, his policy proposals are not dissimilar since he too believes that change can be generated within the existing state framework, not only as a result of conscious political decisions from above but also on the basis of 'oppositional practices' from within generated by state employees. Both Meacher and Walker share a concern which stretches back to Quelch's arguments in Unit 2, namely that it is important for socialists to encourage the development of a locally based, decentralized and democratically controlled social policy as an alternative to bureaucratic administration from above. Another way of viewing the arguments of both Meacher and Walker, however, might be to argue that social policy is more important than ownership of industry or other economic policies. This is, of course, a significant departure not only from the assumptions of Beveridge, but also from many in the socialist tradition (e.g. SDF evidence in Unit 2), by attempting to construct a social policy without *fundamentally* challenging the dominant (capitalist) forms of industrial and commercial organization in society. From this viewpoint, they could be seen as simply attempting to recreated the Fabian tradition in the light of changing (and worse) circumstances.

SAQ Why do you think Friend and Metcalf focus so particularly on children in this extract?

In its social role the state operates in an uneven way providing nothing but a subsistence income for some, giving aid such as housing to others, and in

124

some situations throwing in a whole apparatus of investigation, control and regulation.

This unevenness flows directly out of the cross-class origins of what we now call 'the welfare state'. Its main provisions on social security, pensions, education and health arose out of a convergence of working class demands and the calculations of the more long-sighted political representatives of capital. The latter were also conscious that an educated, healthy and adequately housed workforce would aid post-war growth. Social democracy was the matchmaker and the course of the marriage since then has expressed the strains of the original union.

Although the welfare state emerged from the convergence of the politically articulated demands of distinct classes, it was not the product of an equal partnership between those classes. Working class needs, while recognised, were subsumed into alien institutions which were never under working class control. Capitalist social relations are reproduced through the processes of the welfare state in a number of ways.

The welfare state's institutions and the services they provide are grounded on the view of society which stresses that it is composed of citizens, equal under the law, with mutual rights and obligations. Such a view fragments the working class into either isolated individuals seeking services or special interest groups lobbying for more attention from the state. The state thus relates to the population as 'citizens, voters, taxpayers, patients, social security claimants, employees, smokers, non-smokers, on a host of different bases but never on the basis of class, never on the basis which would raise explicitly the question of exploitation and class domination'. It also reproduces capitalist social relations through the way in which it oversees and intervenes in the family — the cradle of those relations. By looking at the situation of . . . children in care, we will gain a clearer picture of the ways the subordination of the working class is an integral part of the welfare state's activity.

. . . the state's relationship to the family with growing children shows its intervention into working class social life in one of its most developed forms. The architects of the welfare state understood the central importance of the family as the cradle of social relations. The Beveridge report was unambiguous:

> In any measure of social policy in which regard is had to the facts the great majority of married women must be regarded as occupied on work which is vital though unpaid without which their husbands could not do their paid work and without which the whole nation could not continue.

Thereafter while the working class wanted an all round raising of living standards in order to be able to get the most out of married life, the eyes of the state were focusing ever more intently on what was going on inside the family. Truancy, juvenile crime and problem families came up for concerned comment in report after report in the fifties and sixties. The Plowden Report (1960), for example, said: 'It has been recognised that education is concerned with the whole man: henceforth it must be concerned with the whole family'. The state had been buttressing the family with allowances, supplements and free school milk, but now it seemed that a more regulative function was needed. Margaret Wynn, an influential voice of this new orthodoxy, put it this way:

> In the course of a lifetime a well trained man may add £100,000 or sometimes much more to a country's flow of goods and services. Whether or not he does so does not depend only on his education but also upon his upbringing from his early childhood. Some men add little to the wealth of the community, some cost the state thousands of pounds . . . The satisfactory rearing of children may continue to provide its reward for fifty or sixty years.

From all quarters attention was now directed at mothers and their children, by psychologists like Bowlby, the child guidance clinics and educationalists and by the armies of social workers who were being trained in family case work. The social services have come to devote a large proportion of their budgets and their most skilled workers to regulating the reproduction of the next generation of wage labourers.

In its open regulation of family life the welfare state shows itself to be centrally concerned with the reproduction of capitalist social relations. And this concern is evident not only in its most authoritarian and repressive bodies, but in every sphere of its activity. Even in the state's most obviously 'progressive' acts, as when it moves to prevent child battering, it does so in an essentially authoritarian and bureaucratic fashion — denying the rights and needs of the children involved as it resolves the problem institutionally — through children's homes or often randomly assigned foster parents. The network of children's homes has expanded as family and community life has decayed, but the state as parent has proved all too often incapable of meeting the children's emotional needs . . .

The number of children in care has been steadily rising through the sixties and seventies — from 61,600 children in England and Wales in 1959 to 99,600 in 1975. And this increase has been largely a city phenomenon — the percentage of children in the care of county councils was the same, 4.8 per 1,000 of the population under 18 in 1962 as it was in 1973. And once again it is the inner city boroughs which have the highest proportion of children in care. In London, whilst a few middle class suburban boroughs like Richmond actually took proportionally less children into care in 1976 than they did in 1966 (down from 5.2/1,000 to 4.6/1,000), over the same decade, Hackney increased its proportion from 11.4 to 19.2, Lambeth from 12.1 to 20.8 and Camden from 13.3 to 19.2. But the top prizes for vigilance have to go to Kensington and Chelsea with 25.7/1,000 and Tower Hamlets with a staggering 31.5/1,000 in 1976.

These spatial differences arise from two interlocking factors. First, the greater decay of community and family structure in the inner city means that many parents have no one but the state to turn to in critical situations. Thus the most frequent reason for children to be taken into care is the illness or confinement for childbirth of a parent. In the year to April 1975, these reasons caused 2,465 children, out of a total of 6,371, to be taken into care in the Inner London boroughs. Second, it is in the inner city that the crisis has produced the greatest concentration of rebellious youth, the largest numbers of juvenile arrests, a veritable flood of truanting school students — demanding a response from all the institutions of the state from social services to police departments and magistrates courts. But children can be taken into care for far less obvious reasons than these instances of delinquency. There is also growing evidence that social workers are imposing their white middle class values of what a desirable family life should be on urban families who do not fit their stereotypes. In particular, social service departments are keen to investigate one parent families, especially if they are black and the family deviates in any other way from the happy family ideal. There have been a number of cases in London where single parents have approached social service departments for practical help with their children only to find the situation turned on its head — the help they ask denied, and the extreme course of breaking up the family by taking the kids into care to solve 'the problem' pursued.

The social relations established between social services staff and their clients are so permeated with the values of this society that the very act of asking for help defines the client as inadequate and in need of investigation and regulation. In thirty cases investigated by an independent assessment service set up by MIND, the panel agreed with the local authority decision to take the children into care in only three. In particular they considered that councils did not take the cultural background of the families into account. 'If you're trying to define what's in the best interests of children, how do you do it?' asked Ron Lacy of MIND 'What factors do you bring to bear: the expectations of a white middle class family or something else?' . . .

The state, in its welfare aspects, presents us with a familiar dilemma: we need its services for there are no other forces which can intervene to protect children, provide meals on wheels, or supply special schools for disabled children. But its cross-class origins, the bureaucratic framework in which these services operate, their overall strategic orientation, make them at best a distorted shadow of their potential for human liberation — and at worst a cudgel to enforce the sort of social relations government decides are in the best interests of capitalism as a whole. The evolution of the welfare state in the post-war period, the proliferation of its institutions under the control of the professional middle class, tended to reinforce the illusion that the state is a neutral body doing its best to balance conflicting, legitimate interests in a difficult situation . . .

We need a break with an economistic approach to the welfare state which emphasises the need to simply increase the quantity of the services to the working class. We have to challenge the very nature of these services and the ways bureaucratic agencies define, and impose their definition, of the social services' needs of any particular district. We have to raise the question of the local working class defining its own needs — and in that process — redefining the nature of the services which are required.

Within the labour movement itself, it is beginning to be accepted that the mass support for Tory policies at the election and the apathetic response to subsequent economic cuts, indicates the deep disillusionment amongst the working class towards the welfare state. An approach which seeks to maintain the status quo by defending the existing level of services cannot reverse such apathy and hostility. Nor can the problem be overcome by arguing for increased public spending on social services, if the welfare state's features of bureaucracy, control, and regulation of the social life of the working class are not challenged . . .

(Friend and Metcalf, 1981, pp. 136-45)

It seems that the focus on children allows two connected points to be made. First, as feminists have long argued, the family and family ideology play a powerful role in shaping the nature of welfare services. Second, the example is important because it is in relation to children that the idea of welfare as 'care' has been most visible, and Friend and Metcalf are able to contrast that ideal with the practices of the state in controlling children.

They argue that the core of the dilemma is the contrast between the need for welfare and the unfulfilled potential of the welfare state. Our second extract also deals with this tension.

SAQ What strategy does Meacher argue for in addition to the need for 'democratisation from below'?

Socialism with a human face

The capitalist restructuring of the welfare state

. . . All these aspects of the restructuring of the welfare state, have been underpinned by both ideological and eonomic factors which themselves then reinforce the social values of the new right. In terms of the former, they reflect the ideology of self-help, independence and reward for effort that has been systematically propounded over recent years. In terms of the latter, they are linked with a monetarist economic policy that stresses "market forces" (i.e. higher unemployment) and more restrictive industrial relations legislation to discipline the working class and undermine trade union power.

Reversing the subordination of social priorities

[In both the policies of the new right and traditional social democracy,] economic policy is dominant and social equality, social justice and even social integration are subordinated to, even manipulated for, the economic priorities of growth and control of inflation. The 'public burden' model of the social services leads to the national minimum approach, which means that social policy has always been the poor relation both in governmental and consumer terms.

What is needed is a systematic and generalised formulation of social management separate from, though interlinking with, economic management. This is vital when at present the key social policy decisions are taken, not by the cabinet ministers leading the traditional social departments, but by the Chancellor of the Exchequer as a by-product of budget priorities and public expenditure reviews. Treasury dominance is emphasised further by the general vetting procedures for departmental initiatives and by the power of fiscal and monetary policy to determine social structure . . .

To achieve parity, and to ensure that social goals are enmeshed in economic policy-making, social aims must be given equal place with economic aims in the Whitehall institutional framework. Systematic co-ordination between the departments of health and social security, education and science, environment, and the Home Office should be developed on a regularised basis, and reflected in the upgrading of the cabinet sub-committee on social affairs (which should no longer be chaired by the Chancellor). A National Social Development Council should be established to match the NEDC.

Then these new or revamped institutions should be used for consultation prior to fixing budget fiscal, monetary and public expenditure priorities. In addition, this approach must be reinforced ideologically by constant demonstration that the public and social services, so far from constituting a burden on the economy, are indispensable components of successful economic performance.

Democratic reconstruction of services

But it is not just the meshing of social principles within the formulation of economic policy that is needed. It is also essential that both should reflect clear ideological socialist objectives. Now the hallmark of the AES is that it is designed to secure that workers' interests shall prevail over those of capital, and that a central instrument for this purpose are planning agreements that represent a decentralisation of the power of decision-making to the shop floor. This is to be achieved through joint control between management and workers' negotiations at company or plant level over all those issues now outside the scope of collective bargaining — matters of production, investment, manpower planning, product development, buying and selling of industrial assets, etc. — which are at present unilaterally determined by management.

The parallel requirement within the area of social policy is that there should be active and continuous involvement of people in the way public and social services work and in their coverage. In education, for example, this could mean the setting up of schools councils representing teachers, students, parents and ancillary workers, and their involvement in discussions on the content of education, curricula, and systems of examination.

In health, a more effective democratic channel of representation needs to be hammered out between reconstructed Community Health Councils and Area Health Authorities and within the hospitals, which highlights prevention rather than the mystique of curative medicine. In housing, community and tenants' groups should exercise much wider powers of estate management along the lines of many co-operative housing movements.

Positive discrimination for equality of experience

Alongside this the principle of equal access should be pursued. At present there are multiple forms of discrimination in the operation of services in terms of class, sex, age and race as well as income. The raising of charges, the increase in means-testing and the proliferation of selectivity under the Tory new right have all deepened the divide in British society. Our ideological response must be not simply to unwind these divisions by reasserting redistributive taxation, but to set in place programmes of positive discrimination where groups, such as the ethnic minorities, are so disadvantaged that they need supplementary support over and above equal provision.

It is a major task for social policy within the labour movement to mobilise the combined forces of the women's organisations, ethnic minorities and other community bodies to formulate comprehensive programmes that will change the position of women in society, overcome the continuing discrimination experienced by black communities, and radically change the environment for the 16-19 year age group which is now so cruelly deprived.

Equal rights in place of privilege

Perhaps most fundamentally of all, if the AES represents opposition to the power currently enjoyed by national and multi-national capital and a radical shift in the balance of economic power in favour of the working class, then a parallel Alternative *Social* Strategy must involve a comparable programme of social reform. It must achieve an equally radical attack on the traditional privileges of the upper classes and their replacement by a system of well-entrenched civil and social rights extending over the widest area of social and political life.

Such a programme of social reform would include the integration of the public schools, phasing out of private medicine, reform of the Official Secrets Act and replacement by a positive Freedom of Information Act, greater accountability for public bodies such as the police and drastic reform of the present charade of the police complaints procedure, measures to break the monopoly of the press barons and to establish a right of reply under clear conditions for aggrieved members of the public, and other such measures. If these reforms were implemented in a planned and coherent manner, they would bring about a major transformation in the power and privileges of the ruling elites.

It is that, more than anything else, which should form the link between the AES and its necessary corollary, a socialist social strategy.

(Meacher, 1982, pp. 18-21)

Meacher argues that welfare policy has always been a 'poor relation' in terms of government spending and planning, always taking second place to economic planning. He argues that a socialist social policy must be conceived, developed and enacted alongside economic planning to ensure its proper implementation. Our final extract, from Alan Walker, also deals with the priority of welfare policy.

SAQ When reading Walker, you should pay attention to his assessment of the Beveridge welfare state, and the Fabian tradition of planning. What does he argue should replace them?

Why we need a social strategy

What is the Left's social strategy?

The subjugation of social planning to economics follows from the dependence of social policy on economic policy and helps to account for the under-development of social planning in Britain. The main form of social planning is public expenditure planning, or more correctly, public expenditure control. Nationally then social planning is always conducted within the framework of economic planning and what is more, the latter is narrowly interpreted by the Treasury as financial planning. Thus in Britain and other capitalist societies too, the social and economic spheres have been artifically separated and the separation institutionalised through the state's social and economic planning machinery.

Preoccupation with ownership

As well as the economic hegemony which dominates capitalist societies, the failure of the Left to give sufficient attention to social policy must also be attributed in part to the excessive concentration by some Marxists on certain economic relations within the cycle of reproduction. Quite properly emphasis is often placed on the basic structural relations formed within the social division of work: ownership and to a lesser extent power and knowledge. But other relations, such as those formed in the spheres of distribution and consumption, are rarely considered at all. Moreover some of the manifestations of the fundamental relations of production, such as the sexual division of labour and the sort of work that is actually carried out, are similarly not discussed or are made a subsidiary matter for social policy.

My point here is that because of the narrow focus of the AES on ownership of the means of production there is a risk that a change in the ownership of key productive sectors will be taken to be the end of the struggle for socialism. Nothing could be further from the truth. Nationalisation would represent a step towards a socialist economy only if it also entails the replacement of production for profit with production for social need . . .

Planning for social need

The question confronting social planning is can we reform the minimum rights/subsistence approach to welfare which stems from the Beveridge Report and which has characterised the postwar welfare state? The answer is no, because the conception of physical need on which it is based is outmoded and also because it has created and sustained fundamental inequalities, such as the subordinate position of women to men. The economic and ideological functions of the system constructed in the immediate postwar period, including labour discipline, suggest that only limited advances can be secured without a radical re-appraisal of the principles underlying distribution, not only in the public sector but also in the occupational sector. The elimination of widespread poverty and social inequalities rests on the transformation of the systems of production and distribution so that they reflect social need.

This sort of structural change requires democratic control over systems of distribution in *both* of the so-called public and private sectors, that is over the direct distribution of resources through wages, dividends, non-wage benefits and so on, as well as over the redistribution of resources through the tax and social security systems. A 'participation' standard of income could be established which would allow the full participation in family and community life of every individual, regardless of sex and marital status. Income would vary principally on the basis of need, such as family size and disability. Wealth too would be equalised both through the dispersal of the ownership of capital and through increased public ownership under democratic control. Thus for example, housing rights might be shared more equally between owner-occupiers and tenants. Ultimately individual ownership itself would be abolished in favour of local community ownership with the safeguard of strong occupier rights. As a first step the local community might be given the power to restrict certain luxurious forms of owner-occupation and to sub-divide large properties. Large holdings of land would be transferred to the local community. A more progressive wealth and capital gains tax would be required in the short-run.

Planning for need also requires the democratic discussion of an equitable income structure and differentials. A statutory maximum as well as minimum wage may well be another short term option. Collective bargaining at industry and plant level would be circumscribed by these measures and discussions and, following the development of a less hierarchical distribution of incomes, would be more concerned with the social organisation of work than with earnings. A more equitable tax system would accompany changes such as these in the distribution of income. Universal rights to employment, adequate wages, social security, health provision, personal social services, housing and education, coupled with the local democratic control of these institutions, would help to overcome inequalities based on sex and race and also reduce the power of professional groups to control access to these services.

Democratic methods

A major change in the social organisation of health care would also be required under a system aimed at planning for need. This would entail a reorientation of health and welfare services away from institutions towards the community and away from curative medicine towards preventative action. This means a wide range of measures to control drugs, pollution, to reduce accidents and improve diets. It also means less professionally qualified high status jobs and many more less specialised community-based health workers. Private hospitals would be made illegal and the pharmaceutical industry would be strictly controlled. Residential institutions for groups such as the mentally handicapped and elderly would be abolished also, and replaced by smaller nursing units and sheltered purpose-built housing fully integrated with other forms of housing.

These are some of the long term policies towards which a socialist social strategy might be set in order to reduce social inequalities and thereby establish the conditions for socialist evolution. It is according to these social ends that the shape of economic policy and economic planning should be determined. It is, in other words, not a matter of proposing reflation to create more jobs or growth to create more resources, but of asking what are our social goals and which social and economic policies are compatabile with them. Some indication of the scope for redistribution without growth can be guaged from the fact that if the incomes of the top one-tenth of earners were reduced to 75% of their current share, and those of the next two-tenths of 90% of what it is now, this would realise some £19,000 million a year in 1980-81 terms or roughly the amount that was spent in the entire social security programme in that year.

I have described these policies in some detail because this makes it easier to discuss them and any alternatives which might be proposed, as well as the sort of measures necessary in the short and medium term to achieve them. The policies are included for illustrative purposes, it would be quite wrong at this stage to propose a detailed manifesto. As well as having socialist goals, socialist social planning should also employ democratic methods. There have been a series of innovations in planning over the postwar period — including social reports, social accounting, cost benefit analysis, a Department of Economic Affairs and proposals for a Department of Social Planning — all of which have been concerned predominantly with centralised, expert activity and which furthermore, have accepted both the methods and seniority of orthodox economics. In socialist planning goals are inseparable from methods. Utopias elaborated in great detail by experts and imposed on people from above cannot be expected to meet with much success and in the first instance, cannot be expected to attract widespread support at an election.

Oppositional planning

Rather than being an expert or bureaucratic activity, socialist social planning should be diffuse and democratic. Thus social planners would be locally based workers, subject to local control and charged with the task of initiating a planning dialogue. Democratic participation in and control over the planning process is essential also to avoid the growth of corporate power. Thus the social organisation of planning would be an important means of dispersing power. This would entail increased powers for local government in social and economic planning, greater local autonomy and control over resources and devolved powers from local government to smaller geographical areas and groups of citizens.

Socialist social policies of the sort discussed here and a transformative planning system clearly are not compatible with a bourgeois government and state; their introduction therefore rests on the election of a socialist party to power. But the alternative social strategy cannot pin all of its hopes on the election of a Left government. Large sections of the working class are currently oppressed by unemployment, poverty, inequality and powerlessness. Moreover the working class is divided and now is the time to form political alliances to re-establish the common interest between the poor and the rest of the working class. So the planning process must begin at once in a wide range of groups within and outside of the labour movement — trade unions, women's groups, tenants groups, claimants unions and so on — to discuss and formulate socialist policies. Following the election of a socialist government the planning process would be institutionalised by the appointment of social planners and the establishment of local and central planning machinery.

For the present and immediate future our social planning will take an oppositional form as isolated struggles against capitalist institutions and particularly those of the state. Again it is in the realm of the welfare state that these struggles are most frequently manifested but they occur everywhere the contradictions of capitalism are experienced. There is for example, the social security claimants arguing with supplementary benefit officers about their need for money to feed their children and attempting to overcome individualising and demeaning services by gaining common strength, the workers trying to persuade their employer to improve working conditions and the tenants trying to get basic repairs carried out by their landlord.

As well as arguing for an alternative social strategy it may also be possible to *demonstrate* albeit in limited ways, how certain elements of it may work. Professional individuals — doctors, social workers, teachers — can attempt to share power. Similarly in inter-personal relationships. Collectively too there is some scope for the practical demonstration of socialist relations. Some local authorities, such as Sheffield, have begun in recent years to develop small-scale initiatives in socialist planning. Local authorities are also well placed to encourage socialist evolution through for example, the promotion of collective activities such as child care, the reorganisation of services to reflect more directly the needs of citizens and the inclusion of the clients of services in their management. Collective activities can militate against individualism and consumerism.

Socialist social planning is already underway in the form of oppositional struggles against capitalist state institutions and relations. Also in the building of 'oppositional practice' socialists working *within* the state machine are discussing and mentally constructing alternative social relations. The urgent task for the labour movement is to actively support and extend these separate struggles and thereby begin the process of constructing an alternative social strategy, which arises directly out of the experiences of those served by and also those working in state services. It is only when this process is well underway that the Left can have any confidence about the success of the AES in promoting socialist evolution and about the election of a socialist government.

(Walker, 1982, pp. 27, 28-9, 30-1)

Walker argues that the welfare state should be about defining and meeting social need rather than the ideas of physical subsistence upon which Beveridge's proposals were based. Unlike Meacher, he argues that this conception of social policy must in fact lead and direct economic policy. But like Meacher, he believes that these 'central' commitments must also involve democratized forms of planning and control from below.

Friend and Metcalf are most sceptical about the possibilities for change, since they also argue most strongly that the development of social policy has become involved in social control of the poor in the interests of capitalism. They, therefore, emphasize the importance of independent initiatives within the working class which are explicitly counter to existing provision and probably future provision, too.

Meacher is perhaps the least sceptical but he, too, strongly argues both that social policy as a preserve of state experts must change and that the state itself must change giving a new priority to social policy and allowing greater local democratic control over it. Finally, Walker may share some of the fears expressed by Friend and Metcalf, but he outlines in rather more detail how some of the 'democratic' proposals of Meacher might be implemented. In fact, therefore, the view of the state implied by his approach, although theoretically distinct from Meacher's, tends to lead to the same (or similar) policy conclusions.

4.1 CONCLUSION

The fundamental principle of socialist approaches to welfare — that poverty inequality and need are embedded in the capitalist structure of British society — remains a basic starting point. To this has been added a powerful critique of the post-war welfare state. This critique focuses not merely on its 'failures' (e.g. the amount of unmet need) but also questions the very principles on which it was created. Thus socialists argue that the post-war welfare state has not merely to be defended or quantitatively expanded, but radically transformed.

5 IDEOLOGIES AND CONTEMPORARY WELFARE

In some ways, it is not possible to write a definitive conclusion to this unit. The arguments which we have examined here are still active. They are in the process of being developed, and we cannot predict what their future effects on welfare in Britain will be. What is clear, however, is that none of these developments hold out the prospect of a straightforward return to the welfare consensus of 1945 and after.

Since the mid-1970s, this Beveridge–based consensus has become less tenable — economically, politically and ideologically. The contemporary conflict is not about how to rescue this consensus, but over what direction a reconstruction of welfare in Britain should take. The revival of laissez-faire ideology, and its political presence in the new conservatism, has been the most visible challenge to the consensus on welfare. But each of the ideological traditions we have been examining has also been reassessing the welfare politics of 1945 and after.

The welfare state has been a central theme in the revival of **laissez-faire** ideology as a major intellectual and political force. Familiar topics from the history of laissez-faire have made new appearances: particularly the idea of welfare provided by the state, creating dependence and fostering the work shy and scroungers. These effects of 'excessive' welfare have been connected to an economic and political analysis which centres on the status of the welfare state as a monopoly supplier. This status leads to an inefficient, unaccountable, bureaucratic empire, which is a burden on the tax payer and fails to provide the consumer of welfare services with choice. It is important to note that where the person who received welfare services was once spoken of as 'the client' or 'the recipient', he or she is now addressed as 'the consumer'. This change of appellation is not accidental. It points to the way laissez-faire ideology places market relations at the centre of discussions of welfare provision. Their response to state welfare has been to argue for the reduction of state spending and to substitute 'market forces' to provide consumer choice in welfare provision (e.g. through private health insurance). The market, they have argued, promotes individual choice and economic efficiency.

For **Fabianism**, the ideology most closely associated with the post-war welfare state, these attacks on welfare have had profound consequences. As we saw in this unit, Fabianism has tended to fragment — exploring different responses to the future of welfare. Where, in the past, the Fabian belief that a careful examination of the facts about social problems would indicate the rational solution to them, that commitment is now uncertain. Whereas the three extracts we considered in this unit (from Webb, Townsend and Owen) emphasized the need for factual analysis, the conclusions drawn from them led in very divergent policy and political directions. Both Webb and Owen retained something of the Fabian commitment to orthodox policy-making responses, Townsend's conclusions led to a more radical reconsideration of the relation between poverty and the structural distribution of resources.

In a similar way, there are doubts about the political future of Fabianism. Although since the 1920s Fabianism has been associated with the Labour Party, the split within the Labour Party leading to the formation of the SDP has consequences for the future of Fabianism (although not for the Fabian Society). It seems that many elements of The Fabian tradition will be as comfortable in SDP thinking as in the Labour Party.

We suggested that **Socialism** might be taking over something of the role of Fabianism in welfare politics. Certainly there has been a revived interest in the issues of welfare within socialist thinking in recent years, which has placed the connected themes of welfare, need and democratic control very high on the socialist agenda. These themes of social need and democratic control have also provided the basis for a powerful critique of the post-war welfare state, identifying its failure to meet either of these two criteria. Because of this, socialists have moved beyond a purely defensive reaction to the Beveridge-based welfare state, to a developed conception of the need for social planning to meet social need.

One element in the recent development of socialist thinking about welfare has been its greater openness to issues raised by **Feminism**. Recent socialist commentaries (as we saw) have taken questions of sexual inequality and the weight of 'family ideology' in welfare much more seriously. Feminists have maintained their insistence on the failure of welfare to meet the needs of women as independent people, together with a concern that it is through state action that these needs can best be met. Contemporary feminism has linked campaigns about particular welfare issues to a wider analysis of the way welfare ideologies and practice have reinforced the subordination of women. They have had the sharpest understanding of the *prescriptive* character of welfare, particularly the persistent assumption that women are necessarily economically dependent on men. But they have also maintained the argument that it is through reformed state welfare that social needs can best be met, and have conducted substantial campaigns around specific welfare legislation. In recent years, they have particularly identified the ways in which the reduction of welfare provision by the state is likely to bear very heavily on women, and have pointed to the manner in which this reduced commitment to welfare has been accompanied by a campaign to reassert the traditional conception that a woman's proper place is in the home.

As we write (April, 1983) the future of welfare in Britain is uncertain. The welfare consensus is in disarray, and very divergent strategies for the reconstruction of welfare are available. What is certain is that the future of welfare will emerge from within the field of ideologies that we have considered in these units. In Units 2 and 3 we examined how these ideologies were enmeshed in the development of the British welfare state. In this unit, we have examined their responses to the 'crisis of welfare' from the mid-1970s. Which of them will emerge as the dominant force in the second half of the 1980s remains an open question.

6 ANALYSING IDEOLOGIES OF WELFARE

At this point, it would be useful for you to read the article by Phil Lee and Colin Raban 'Welfare and ideology' in the Course Reader. In this article, Lee and Raban examine some of the problems associated with the use of 'ideology' in studying social policy. They trace the development of attempts to classify different ideologies of welfare and offer some criticisms of these classifications. In doing so, they point to some limitations in the use of the concept of ideology in these attempts at classification.

SAQ When reading the article, you should try to:

1 Assess the criticisms of attempts to classify ideologies of welfare, in particular their claim that such classifications must include the dimension of control.

2 Assess their argument that ideology must refer to more than a system of ideas about welfare. In particular, you should pay attention to their argument that welfare provision and practice embodies specific ideological assumptions. They also suggest that it is important to consider ideologies as active social and political *forces* in which real conflicts are fought out.

In reading the article, you will have seen that Lee and Raban draw explicit attention to points which we have treated relatively implicitly within our discussion of the four ideologies of welfare in these units. For example, within the ideologies, we have considered the ways in which they identify issues of choice, freedom, control and democracy. Lee and Raban provide an important reminder that ideologies of welfare differ not only in *what* welfare they think should be provided but also *how* (through what means) it should be available. The question of means is as central a political issue as the question of the content of welfare.

They also point to the significance of understanding welfare provision as containing prescriptive ideological assumptions. We have seen in the course of our history of welfare ideologies, that this issue has persistently attracted the attention of feminist and socialist critics of welfare, who have identified the moral and ideological assumptions contained within the existing array of welfare provision.

7 THEORY AND POLITICS IN THE 'CRISIS OF WELFARE'

Lee and Raban's argument that ideologies have to be understood as politically active forces leads us to a further set of issues. In Unit 1, you read Chapter 1 of Ramesh Mishra's book. There he identified how theoretical arguments about welfare had become increasingly politicized. In Chapters 2 and 3 of the book he examines two approaches to the welfare state which connect with two of the ideologies we have considered in this block: 'neo-conservatism' and 'Marxism'.

Because of Mishra's explicitly contemporary focus, we feel that the end of this unit is the most satisfactory point at which to read these two chapters. They add a rather different approach to our presentation of contemporary laissez-faire and socialist ideologies of welfare. Mishra's approach is different in two main respects.

First, where Units 2-4 have examined the development of political ideologies of welfare, placing emphasis on the *political* arguments, Mishra examines the intellectual or *theoretical* structure of the different approaches before considering their political implications. That is, he begins from the more abstract or academic form of these arguments.

Second, where these units have attempted to present the different ideologies and allow you to make comparisons between them, Mishra's book is organized around providing an *evaluative commentary* on these approaches. That is, Mishra examines the arguments put forward and subjects them to criticism. It is important when reading these chapters (and subsequent ones) to remember that this criticism is not itself abstract — or divorced from the politics of theory. Mishra too has a position which he wants to *argue for*. This position, as will become clear in reading the whole of the set book, informs and shapes the sorts of criticisms he offers of other positions.

7.1 EVALUATING NEO-CONSERVATISM

In Chapter 2, Mishra considers the development of neo-conservatism, and examines the economic and political arguments which have provided the intellectual support for its attack on the welfare consensus. He also considers the practice of two governments influenced by neo-conservative theories.

SAQ   When reading Chapter 2, you should try to:

1   Identify neo-conservative explanations of 'government failure'.

2   Identify why the welfare state is so central to these arguments.

3   Examine the alternative view of welfare and the state provided by the neo-conservatives; and

4   Assess Mishra's evaluation of neo-conservative theory and political practice.

Mishra suggests that neo-conservative theory has developed around two main issues: one political, the other economic. In political terms, they have argued that contemporary government is 'overloaded' by competing demands from diverse interest groups in the 'political market'. This, they suggest, has led to an unchecked growth in government, particularly in the field of welfare. This uncontrolled development is connected with another form of government 'failure'. Intervention, they suggest, was developed to correct the 'failings' of the market economy, but government intervention has proved to be just as fallible, without the disciplines of the market. That is, government has been fallible and uncontrolled.

For the neo-conservatives, these two elements lead to the economic consequences of government intervention: a distortion of the workings of supply and demand in the market; increasing money supply to finance government debt, thus causing inflation.

Their central argument (as we have seen in the previous units) is that the state should withdraw and allow the free play of market forces to be restored in many areas of social life, particularly in the field of social welfare.

Mishra's commentary on neo-conservatism raises some interesting points. He suggests

1   they are incorrect in their identification of 'deficit financing' as the major cause of inflation and economic recession;

2   that, in practice, neo-conservatives have found 'government overload' very difficult to manage, and that this 'political market' is a structural and necessary feature of contemporary democratic politics;

3   that the 'failure' of government welfare programmes involves a misunderstanding of social problems and possible solutions. He suggests that they have taken the ideology of 'social engineering' too seriously, and that the reality of social and political organization is necessarily more complex than the idea of 'social engineering' allows.

7.2 EVALUATING MARXISM

In Chapter 3, Mishra considers Marxist analyses of welfare, and discusses their political implications. When reading this chapter, you should pay attention to some divergences between Mishra's presentation of Marxism (as an academic theory) and the presentation of socialist arguments for welfare in this block (particularly in Unit 4).

1   identify the main arguments of the Marxist analysis of welfare;

2   identify what Mishra says about the political implications of these analyses;

3   assess Mishra's criticisms of the Marxist approach to welfare.

Mishra adds to the arguments we have already considered about the functions of welfare reform in maintaining and legitimating capitalism. He discusses the ideas of class struggle over welfare, and the conception of the welfare state as contradictory, as a consequence of being created out of conflicting class interests. These analyses, he suggests, provide a powerful understanding of the development of the welfare state. However, he suggests that although Marxism provides one of the most powerful theoretical means of analysing welfare, its political implications are far less satisfactory. He suggests that Marxist politics are trapped between the image of 'actually existing' socialism (in Eastern Europe) and 'utopian socialism'. Consequently, he suggests, marxists tend to be left in a merely 'defensive' posture in the face of cuts in the welfare state, with no real politics of welfare of their own. You should consider whether the socialist arguments for welfare presented in this unit fit Mishra's description of Marxist politics of welfare. In particular, Mishra seems to have little to say about the theme of democratic control which we have seen as one of the central themes of socialist ideologies of welfare.

7.3 IDEOLOGIES AND SOCIAL POLICY

You will be reading further chapters of Mishra's book in subsequent units. Among these will be his consideration of the Fabian approach to welfare. When reading the remainder of the book, you should note one other major difference from the discussion of welfare ideologies in this block. Mishra does not consider Feminism as a separate theory and politics of welfare. When reading the rest of Mishra, you should try to assess what consequences this absence has for the arguments he puts forward. In this block, we have suggested that Feminism has provided a distinctive set of analyses, criticisms and demands around welfare. Is something of importance lost if these issues are not considered in the study of welfare? This problem will be taken up again when you read the last chapter of Mishra's book in Unit 16 of the course.

In this block, we have focused primarily on the political ideologies of welfare. This may seem a considerable distance from the study of particular issues and policies in social welfare. We hope that these units have demonstrated how profoundly the development of the British welfare state has been bound up with these conflicting ideologies. We also hope that in the remainder of the course you will discover how these ideologies intersect with a variety of issues in social welfare. Welfare policy is *never* a purely technical matter, it always connects with wider social currents and conflicts.

REFERENCES

ANDERSON, D., LAIT, J. and MARSLAND, D. (1977) *Breaking the Spell of the Welfare State,* Social Affairs Unit of the Centre for Policy Studies.

CLAIMANTS' UNION (1982) *Women and Social Security,* pamphlet published by the Claimants' Union.

COUSSINS, J. and COOTE, A. (1981) *The Family in the Firing Line,* a joint Child Poverty Action Group/National Council for Civil Liberties publication.

FLEMING, S. (1973) *The Family Allowance Under Attack,* pamphlet from the Family Allowance Campaign, Bristol, Falling Wall Press.

FRIEND, A. and METCALF, A. (1981) *Slump City,* London, Pluto Press.

JOSEPH, K. (1977) *Monetarism Is Not Enough,* London, Centre for Policy Studies.

LEE, P. and RABAN, C. (1983) 'Welfare and ideology', in LONEY, M., BOSWELL, D. and CLARKE, J. (eds) *Social Policy and Social Welfare,* Milton Keynes, The Open University Press (Course Reader) pp. 18-32.

McINTOSH, M. (1981) 'Feminism and social policy', *Critical Social Policy,* Vol. 1, No. 1, pp. 32-41.

MEACHER, M. (1982) 'Socialism with a human face', *New Socialist,* No. 4, March/April.

MISHRA, R. (1983) *The Welfare State in Crisis,* Brighton, Harvester Press (Set book).

OWEN, D. (1981) *Face the Future,* London, Jonathan Cape.

SELDON, A. (1977) *Charge!,* London, Temple Smith.

TOWNSEND, P. (1979) *Poverty in the United Kingdom,* Harmondsworth, Penguin.

WALKER, A. (1982) 'Why we need a social strategy', *Marxism Today,* September.

WEBB, A. (1980) 'The personal social services', in BOSANQUET, N. and TOWNSEND, P. (eds) *Labour and Equality,* London, Heinemann.

ACKNOWLEDGEMENTS

Grateful acknowledgement is made to the following sources for material used in this unit:

Text

Policy Studies Institute for K. Joseph, *Monetarism is Not Enough,* 1976; The Social Affairs Unit for D. Anderson *et al., Breaking the Spell of the Welfare State,* 1977; Maurice Temple Smith for A. Seldon, *Charge,* 1977, first published in Great Britain by Maurice Temple Smith; M. McIntosh for her article 'Feminism and Social Policy' in *Critical Social Policy,* vol. 1, no. 1, 1981; National Council for Civil Liberties for J. Coussins and A. Coote, *The Family in the Firing Line,* 1981; Heinemann Educational Books for A. Webb, 'The personal social services' in Bosanquet, N. and Townsend, P. (eds) *Labour and Equality,* 1980; Penguin Books and University of California Press for P. Townsend, *Poverty in the United Kingdom,* 1979, © Peter Townsend; Jonathan Cape and Praeger Publishers for D. Owen, *Face the Future,* 1981, © 1981 David Owen, reprinted and abridged by permission; Pluto Press for A. Friend and A. Metcalf, *Slump City,* 1981; *New Socialist* for M. Meacher, 'Socialism with a human face', no. 4, March/April, 1982; Alan Walker for his article 'Why we need a social strategy' in *Marxism Today,* September, 1982.

Illustrations

p. 93 Topix; *p. 109* Cath Jackson; *pp. 114 and 115* Fabian Society.